Teaching Mathematically Able Children

SECOND EDITION

Roy Kennard

David Fulton Publishers

London

in association with

The National Association for Able Children in Education

David Fulton Publishers Ltd
The Chiswick Centre, 414 Chiswick High Road, London W4 5TF
www.fultonpublishers.co.uk

First published in Great Britain in 1996 by David Fulton Publishers

Note: The rights of Roy Kennard to be identified as the authors of this work
have been asserted by them in accordance with the Copyright, Designs and
Patents Act 1988.

David Fulton Publishers is a division of Granada Learning Limited, part of
Granada plc.

British Library Cataloguing in Publication Data
A catalogue record for this book is available from the British Library.

ISBN 1-85346-798-7

Typeset by Kate Williams
Printed and bound in Great Britain

Contents

To Barbara, Ben and Julia

Preface to second edition

At the time of writing the first edition of *Teaching Mathematically Able Children* I wondered about the depth of interest in this particular field of mathematics education. It never occurred to me that I might be introducing a second edition! A lot has happened in the past five years to create a broadly receptive climate for discussions about provision for very able pupils. Initiatives like the National Numeracy Strategy (NNS), Excellence in Cities (EiC) and the Qualifications and Curriculum Authority's (QCA) Gifted and Talented Exemplification Project all recognise the needs of this particular group of children. The National Association for Able Children in Education (NACE) and similar organisations continue to keep able pupils on the political and educational agenda. Yet there is still much to do. Once again, I hope this book will be of practical assistance to teachers designing and teaching programmes targeted at mathematically able pupils.

Roy Kennard
May 2001

Acknowledgements

I would like to thank the pupils, teachers and professional colleagues who helped me with the preparation of the first edition of this book. In this regard I am especially grateful to pupils from primary and secondary schools in Sunderland, Michael Chyriwsky, Deborah Eyre, Peter Smith, Christine Taylor, Ron Thompson and Brian Weller. Thanks also to Johanna Raffan for encouraging me to undertake this revised and updated second edition.

THE NATIONAL ASSOCIATION FOR
ABLE CHILDREN IN EDUCATION
PO Box 242, Arnolds Way,
Oxford OX2 9FR

Registered Charity No 327230

Tel: 01865 861879
e-mail: info@nace.co.uk

Fax: 01865 861880
www.nace.co.uk

MISSION STATEMENT

NACE . . . the association of professionals, promoting and supporting the education of able and talented children.

AIMS

1. To promote the fact that able and talented children have particular educational needs that must be met to realise their full potential.
2. To be proactive in promoting discussion and debate by raising appropriate issues in all education forums and through liaison with educational policy makers.
3. To encourage commitment to the personal, social and intellectual development of the whole child.
4. To encourage a broad, balanced and appropriate curriculum for able and talented children.
5. To encourage the use of a differentiated educational provision in the classroom through curriculum enrichment and extension.
6. To make education an enjoyable, exciting and worthwhile experience for the able and talented child.

OBJECTIVES

1. To promote the development, implementation and evaluation in all schools of a coherent policy for able and talented children.
2. To provide appropriate support, resources and materials for the education of able and talented children.
3. To provide methods of identification and support to the education community.
4. To provide and facilitate appropriate initial teacher training.
5. To stimulate, initiate and coordinate research activities.
6. To develop a national base and establish regional centres.

STATEMENT

To make education an enjoyable, exciting and worthwhile experience for able and talented children.

Introduction

There has been a long-standing and well-documented concern about provision in our schools for mathematically able children (Her Majesty's Inspectorate of Schools (HMI) 1978, 1979, 1992; Office for Standards in Education (OFSTED) 1994, 1995, 1998, 1999a; Department for Education and Employment (DfEE) 2000a). The central issue to emerge from these reports is that all too often able children are 'insufficiently challenged by the work they are set' (HMI 1992: vii). The aims of this book are thus twofold: first, to provide teachers wishing to respond to this concern with an analysis of the relevant issues; and, secondly, to offer practical strategies for teachers seeking to provide challenging mathematical experiences for their most able pupils.

It is possible to argue, however, that all pupils should be challenged, and not just the most able. In this context OFSTED has raised as a key issue for schools the provision of sufficient challenge for pupils of all abilities (1995: 5). With this last point in mind, many of the practical approaches discussed in this book are relevant to a wider group of pupils. There is evidence to suggest that where schools do focus on their provision for the most able it has the consequence of generally raising expectations, and in some schools this leads to improved exam results (HMI 1992: viii).

Many reports and studies comment on the difficulty of defining the very able or gifted child. HMI expressed this as:

> There is no generally accepted definition of what constitutes a very able or gifted child. (1992: 1)

It is not unusual, however, to try to achieve a definition of sorts by attempting to quantify the proportions of children in these categories in terms of the top 5% or 10% of the ability range. Some researchers argue for a wider proportion on the grounds that errors abound in any identification process. In other words, we must be cautious about specifying cut-off points, but there is also a sense in which identification need not be the precursor to provision. Since it is possible to argue that *all* children should be challenged, not just the most able, a case can be made for trying to identify able children in terms of their *response to challenge* (Straker 1983). The most able are thus recognisable in terms of the strength of the aptitudes that they display.

There seems to be a case for characterising able pupils in terms of the mathematical abilities that they display. HMI expressed a similar sentiment when they commented that:

> Schools use a variety of methods to identify the very able. However, it is rare to find use being made of subject-specific criteria. (1992: viii)

Further impetus for the development of a view about the mathematical characteristics of able children comes from a secondary school head of mathematics, who, in response to a question about provision in his department, said, 'it all depends on how *discerning* the teacher is'. In other words, what we notice and subsequently provide depends on the interpretive framework that we employ.

An alternative approach, which has gained ground recently, is to define able pupils in terms of National Curriculum levels. However, a major thrust of this book is to examine ways in which teachers can be more *discerning* in their own classrooms. It will be argued that the *recognition* of mathematical ability goes hand in hand with its *development*. This is a day-to-day process, going well beyond the notion of a classification in percentage terms.

The issue of what teachers can look out for provides the focus for Chapter 1. Are there grounds for a subject-specific approach? Does the nature of mathematical thinking provide any clues? The outcomes of a major study in this area are summarised and other research is reviewed. Chapter 2 uses the National Curriculum for Mathematics (DfEE/Qualifications and Curriculum Authority (QCA) 1999) and the NNS Frameworks (DfEE 1999, 2001) as standpoints for viewing the characteristic abilities of able children. Are the abilities discussed in Chapter 1 reflected in the programmes of study at each Key Stage? In Chapter 3, pupils' self-perceptions of the mathematical methods they employ are interpreted in terms of the emerging structure of mathematical abilities.

In Chapter 4 an overarching strategy for provision is put forward. With a view of what it means to be mathematically able in mind, what kind of teaching methods and resources will extend the abilities of able pupils? Complementary organisational approaches are discussed in Chapter 5, in particular the issue of how best to design a challenging mathematics curriculum.

Chapters 6–8 present three case studies in which pupils' work is interpreted in the light of the structure of abilities formulated. Work of this kind is seen as an essential way for teachers to achieve a shared understanding of the most appropriate forms of provision for able pupils.The remaining chapters briefly discuss the issue of gender differences in mathematical achievement and possible resources for a challenging mathematics curriculum.

In summary, this book seeks to develop a greater understanding among teachers of mathematics about the most appropriate ways of providing a challenging curriculum for their most able pupils.

Chapter 1

Perspectives on the characteristic mathematical abilities of able children

A starting point for the exploration of mathematical ability is the consideration of the nature of mathematics itself. The *content* of the school mathematics curriculum is recognisable to most people. In this sense we know what mathematics looks like. We recognise the facts, skills and conceptual structures that make up *number, algebra, geometry* and *statistics*. Facts are generally regarded as items of knowledge that must be remembered, while skills are seen as procedures that improve with practice. Both are embedded in a richly interconnecting network or conceptual structure (Cockcroft 1982). Typically, it is this content that is assessed through the traditional forms of testing and examining, and for many people this content is the mathematics. While this view of mathematics is popular it is also restrictive. In terms of throwing light on the nature of mathematical ability it is not very helpful.

A sound complementary case can be made for seeing mathematics as something more than pure content. The key point here is that mathematics may be viewed as an activity or as a set of interrelated processes. From this standpoint the content of mathematics is the outcome of this activity. The nature of this activity is readily revealed through reflection on the processes involved in creating mathematics at a personal level. That is to say, if the mathematical task is essentially one of problem solving or enquiry then stepping back from the mathematics itself and reflecting on the strategies involved will illuminate the nature of mathematical thinking. The key processes revealed by working in this way appear to be: searching for and recognising pattern; specialising; conjecturing; representing, including the use of symbols and diagrams; generalising; verifying; and proving (Bell *et al.* 1979; Mason 1985; Pirie 1987). If the processes referred to here are essential to *making* mathematics, can they also be regarded as abilities?

Two further questions arise at this point. First, is the picture complete yet? Has the full range of abilities been articulated? Secondly, do mathematically able children show such abilities to a greater

Mathematics as an activity

degree than their relatively less able peers? If so, will a complete picture of the nature of mathematical ability help teachers in ordinary classrooms to identify mathematically able children?

The work of Krutetskii

Recent studies and sources of debate about provision for mathematically able children have all drawn on the work of V. A. Krutetskii (1976). This was a major study lasting 12 years that set out to describe the characteristics of 'mathematically gifted pupils as they solve various problems' (p. 78). His aim was to identify aspects of mathematical ability 'in which differences between pupils capable of learning mathematics and pupils less capable would be the most striking' (p. 84). Typically it is Krutetskii's conclusions that are referred to rather than the way he constructed his model of mathematical ability. He reveals that this was done by making certain assumptions, through initial probing experiments and observations of gifted primary school children and by reflecting on the essence of mathematical thinking. Table 1.1 summarises Krutetskii's model in these terms.

In developing his theory of logical-mathematical intelligence Gardner (1993) also sought to characterise mathematical ability by examining the essence of mathematics and the work of eminent mathematicians. His conclusions closely resemble many of the characteristics above, most notably: sensing the direction of a problem; sustaining long chains of reasoning; using mathematical notation;

Table 1.1 Structure of mathematical abilities (A, assumption; E, essence of mathematical thinking; O, observation)

Able children have the ability to:	Basis for inclusion in the model
Grasp the formal structure of a problem in a way that leads to ideas for action.	A, O, E
Generalise from the study of examples. Generalise approaches to problem solving.	A, E
Reason in a logical way and as a consequence develop chains of reasoning.	E
Use mathematical symbols as part of the thinking process.	E
Think flexibly; adapt their ways of approaching problems and to switch from one mode of thought to another.	O
Reverse their direction of thought. Work forwards and backwards in an attempt to solve a problem.	A
Leave out intermediate steps in a logical argument and think in abbreviated mathematical forms.	A
Remember generalised mathematical relationships, problem types, generalised ways of approaching problems and patterns of reasoning.	A

specialising or breaking down a problem into simpler but related parts; abstracting general features from mathematical material; and remembering general arguments based on mathematical reasoning.

Krutetskii then devised a series of tests in which the abilities hypothesised reflected a view of problem solving corresponding to the three stages of interpreting, processing and retaining information. Analysis of the results of these tests confirmed the hypothetical model. He also found that capable pupils typically searched for the simplest or most economical solution and saw this as a consequence of the ability to think flexibly. Gifted pupils also exhibit a 'mathematical cast of mind', which enables them to view the world mathematically. This takes the form of a tendency to think in visual–spatial terms, logical–analytical terms or both. The abilities for visualising mathematical forms and for spatial concepts are not integral to Krutetskii's structure of mathematical abilities; he regards them only as indicators of a particular type of mind. In this context other researchers have found that pupils with a tendency to visualise mathematical material are under-represented in groups of high mathematical achievers (Presmeg 1986). Krutetskii also omits speed of thought, computational ability and a memory for numbers, symbols and formulae from his model. They might be useful but they do not characterise only the most capable pupils. With regard to memory, Krutetskii is clear that able pupils are characterised by a capacity to remember generalised approaches and patterns of reasoning rather than a capacity for the pure recall of specific information.

The structure developed by Krutetskii is a consequence of the responses of able and relatively less able children to his test items. His model seems to confirm the process abilities mentioned above, although not always in quite the same terms. The process of proving, for example, clearly relates to his component about the ability to reason logically. The process of generalising maps onto Krutetskii's category of the same name, but Krutetskii goes further with references to generalised approaches to problem solving. The processes of searching for pattern through the exploration of special cases leading to conjectures about possible relationships seems to correspond to his point about generalising from the study of examples. Symbolising or the use of symbols is a feature of mathematical activity and appears as an element of Krutetskii's model. Other research by Osborn (1983) suggests that mathematically able children are recognisable by their ability to manipulate symbolic representations of abstract quantities.

There does seem to be a case, however, for making these process abilities explicit and not subsuming them into Krutetskii's categories. Specialising, for example, is the generating of examples for further study, and is best carried out systematically to reveal patterns. International research supports the view that mathematically gifted pupils have the ability to work systematically (Span and Overtoom-Corsmit 1986). Mason describes conjecturing as the 'recognising of a burgeoning generalisation' (1985: 82) and it may be seen as the process of articulating possible relationships, and is thus associated with the

3

supporting processes of checking and verifying. This area of overlap between Krutetskii's abilities and the notion of process abilities occurs because of attempts to describe the essence of mathematical thinking. The structure put forward by Krutetskii is, however, wider than the notion of process abilities arrived at by reflecting on mathematics as an activity.

Age

Krutetskii also considers the development of mathematical abilities with respect to age. The model of mathematical abilities referred to in Table 1.1 seems to be associated with able children of secondary school age. In the primary years, however, children as young as 8 years old may show embryonic forms of these components of mathematical ability. Krutetskii observed that with appropriate teaching children's embryonic forms develop noticeably between the ages of 8 and 10. In seeking to describe the characteristic abilities of able children in the primary years he excluded exceptionally gifted children and did not attempt to 'strictly' relate specific characteristics to specific ages. His analysis focused on the characteristic abilities of generalising, perceiving the formal structure of a problem, curtailment of thinking, flexibility of thinking, striving for elegant solutions and mathematical memory.

The ability to generalise emerges earlier than other components of mathematical ability. Initially this takes the form of a child being able to recognise an instance of a general rule. Krutetskii observed that children exhibited the ability to work from particular cases towards an unknown general rule only from about the age of 11. The ability to generalise is closely associated with the ability to perceive formally the essence of mathematical material. Children as young as 8 years old can focus on the relationships between quantities without being held by the nature of the concrete objects involved. Less able pupils see only the objects, and not the relationships between them.

Curtailment of reasoning only appears in a rudimentary form in the primary years. Difficult problems are solved step by step. Some curtailment was noticed in the thinking of capable 9- and 10-year-olds, especially where there was familiarity with the problem type. Flexibility of thinking in terms of searching for alternative ways of solving problems was not observed in the thinking of 8-year-olds. The only exception to this was when researchers intervened, and in these instances children aged 8–10 did show signs of flexibility. Older children with a capability for mathematics demonstrate flexibility when they independently make fresh approaches to mathematical material and show that they are not limited by previous methods.

The tendency to search for the simplest or most economical solution to a problem is not a characteristic of able children in the primary years. Only from the age of about 11 onwards do able children exhibit this particular ability. Krutetskii also reports that for the primary years he did not observe a tendency for children to remember generalised approaches and patterns of reasoning. Children in these years tend to remember generalised results and the specifics of a mathematical situation. During the primary years children tend to remember both the 'general and the particular, the relevant and the irrelevant, the necessary and the unnecessary' (Krutetskii 1976: 339). Older children will tend to remember generalised approaches in such a way that if a result is forgotten it can be reconstructed.

For views on the characteristics of children in the infant years Straker (1983) reports the observations of teachers. Mathematical ability manifests itself in:

> A liking for numbers including use of them in stories and rhymes; an ability to argue, question and reason using logical connectives: if, then, so, because, either, or . . .; pattern-making revealing balance or symmetry; precision in positioning toys, e.g. cars set out in ordered rows, dolls arranged in order of size; use of sophisticated criteria for sorting and classification; pleasure in jigsaws and other constructional toys. (1983: 17)

It is important to note that some of the above points do not entirely correspond to Krutetskii's model. Characteristics associated with 'liking' and 'pleasure' are of a qualitatively different kind to the features of ability so far discussed. While able children may show these traits they cannot be thought of as abilities. Sorting and classifying, however, may be seen as activities linked to generalising. They promote discrimination between objects in order to make general classifications.

Further teacher observations are reported by Straker, although the age group is unspecified, and once again these are a mixture of attitudes, character traits and abilities. Extracting only the references to ability in these teacher observations gives a picture of mathematical ability that emphasises flexibility and mathematical justification. Flexibility is described in terms of looking for alternative approaches and searching for the simplest solution. Mathematical justification is referred to in terms of reasoning from evidence. Able children are also described as frequently inquisitive in a mathematical way about the world in which they live; in Krutetskii's terms they exhibit a 'mathematical cast of mind'.

Recent guidance from the NNS, targeted at primary school teachers, says of mathematically able pupils that:

> They typically:
> - grasp new material quickly;
> - are prepared to approach problems from different directions and persist in finding solutions;
> - generalise patterns and relationships;
> - use mathematical symbols confidently;
> - develop concise logical arguments. (DfEE 2000b: 4)

Other guidance emanating from the National Literacy and Numeracy Strategies offers a similar model but adds that:

> Pupils who are able in mathematics:
> - develop logical arguments, often taking valid shortcuts;
> - may not be exceptional in carrying out calculations, but may see calculations as detail and less important than the problem as a whole. (DfEE 2000c: 2)

The NNS guidance does not distinguish between different year groups in the primary age phase. In this regard it seems to be suggesting that when pupils display the characteristics mentioned they may be regarded as more able in mathematics irrespective of their age. The NNS guidance clearly overlaps with Krutetskii's profile of abilities but, in a similar way to Straker's analysis, it also incorporates traits such as 'persistence'. It concurs with Krutetskii in that it does not see computational ability as an indicator of high mathematical ability but departs from his model for children under the age of 11 by including speed of thought, logical argument and the confident use of mathematical symbols. It must be remembered, however, that Krutetskii restricted his age-related study and that he avoided a tight mapping between specific ages and specific abilities for pupils in the primary age phase. Support for the wider NNS view, which incorporates these additional features from Krutetskii's model, can be found in Chapter 7, which reports a case study into the mathematical behaviour of able Year 6 pupils.

A large-scale survey of secondary school mathematics teachers' perceptions of able children revealed strong support for features of Krutetskii's model of abilities (Chyriwsky and Kennard 1997). Questionnaire returns were received from 524 teachers in 355 schools with over 80 per cent of teachers indicating their agreement that significant characteristics of mathematically able children are:

- ability to make generalisations from the study of examples;
- logical reasoning;
- rapid grasp of new material;
- ability to justify results and relationships;
- ability to grasp the formal structure of a problem;
- flexibility (employ different methods in search of a solution);
- curtailed reasoning (takes valid shortcuts towards the solution);
- ability to use symbols to represent relationships and quantities;
- ability to reverse mathematical processes (1997: 55).

A 'memory for mathematical rules and results' attracted the agreement of only 60 per cent of the sample. This may be because some teachers interpreted this item in terms of a pure recall facility without any associated understanding. Although 'the rapid grasp of new material' was seen as a key characteristic by this group of teachers and is also referred to in the NNS guidance, it was not seen as essential by Krutetskii. The following comments from the same survey reveal in the words of the teachers themselves how they see the mathematical characteristics of able children. They say that able children:

- have 'a much clearer mental picture and develop an ability to stand back from a task and view it from alternative angles';
- have an 'intuitive grasp of the direction of a problem';
- have 'an ability to see a pattern and exploit it';
- have the 'ability to find flaws in chains of reasoning';
- 'use ... abstract algebra [and have] skill and confidence in manipulation of algebraic expressions';
- have the 'ability to find more than one way to solve a problem';
- have the 'ability to find and solve problems when none are indicated; i.e. a willingness to look for mathematical problems/ideas in everyday life';
- have an 'intuitive grasp of relationships'.

The references to intuitive approaches are interesting. The role of intuition in the solution of mathematical problems was investigated by Krutetskii, who explained the phenomenon in terms of a child's previous mathematical experience and in particular an ability to generalise and an ability to think in curtailed structures.

Other research has also utilised Krutetskii's model, most notably that of Denton and Postlethwaite (1985), who devised a checklist for the identification of children with high mathematical ability. Using Krutetskii's structure of abilities and background work of their own they developed tests for each of the 22 items in their checklist. When these tests were given to a group of children aged 13–14 years old with high mathematical ability and a group of children of average ability, the high ability group achieved higher scores on each of the ability categories. Their checklist includes the item 'Can perform any arithmetical computation accurately and with ease' (1985: 38), suggesting that this is a characteristic ability of able children, but this is at odds with both Krutetskii and the NNS guidance.

General or specific

Are the abilities identified above specific to mathematics or simply derivatives of a more general form of ability? Do children with a high general ability also tend to exhibit high mathematical ability? But what is meant here by general ability? There is a long history of interpreting general ability to mean 'intelligence'. However, it is clear from the literature in this field that there is no agreed definition of what constitutes intelligence. Intelligence is not any one thing and it certainly is not a number! For example, Gardner (1983) argues that our abilities are best viewed as comprising a set of 'multiple intelligences' of which 'logical-mathematical' intelligence is one; the others are identified as linguistic, spatial, musical, bodily-kinaesthetic, interpersonal and intrapersonal.

Intelligence test scores or intelligence quotient (IQ) scores do, however, correlate with performance in school subjects (Freeman 1998:

7). They are useful, therefore, for identifying academically able pupils but some caution still needs to be exercised. For example, Renzulli states that 'Because IQ scores correlate only from 0.4 to 0.6 with school grades, they account for only 16–36% of the variance in these indicators of potential' (1986: 58). In other words, success in school subjects depends on a range of factors other than the general ability inferred from an IQ score. Krutetskii also considered this issue and, with respect to the ability to generalise, concluded that although this was a feature of general ability, the ability to 'generalise numerical and spatial relations, expressed in number and letter symbolism' (1976: 353) is a specific mathematical ability. He reached this conclusion after studying how well a group of primary school children generalised mathematical and non-mathematical material. This study showed that capable mathematicians generalised mathematical material at a high level. On a scale of 1–5, with 5 representing the highest level, the capable mathematicians generalised at level 5 but occasionally dropped to level 3 on non-mathematical material. Chil–dren who were regarded as relatively incapable at mathematics generalised mathematical material at level 1 but in generalising non-mathematical material occasionally achieved level 4.

The relevance of this discussion becomes apparent when practical decisions associated with provision need to be made. Should we think of children as generally able or having specific abilities that need to be nurtured? Support for a subject-specific approach to the teaching of able children comes from the results of a study in which teacher nomination and testing were used to identify the top 10% of Year 9 pupils in four different subjects (Denton and Postlethwaite 1985). The study covered 11 schools and approximately 2300 pupils and found that only a small proportion of pupils, 12% of those nominated by teachers and 15% of those identified through testing, were considered as high ability in all four subjects. Of those selected to be in the top 10% for mathematics, only 53% were also selected by the same method for English, 45% for French and 66% for physics. Reflecting on their data the researchers go on to conjecture that if a smaller ability band was selected (less than 10%), or the number of subjects was increased beyond four, '*very* small numbers' of pupils would appear in categories showing high ability in all subjects (1985: 26).

Ways of grouping pupils, especially in secondary schools, will also to some extent be influenced by views about the nature of human abilities. A preference for a subject-specific approach is confirmed in the survey of secondary mathematics teachers mentioned above. The study found that 91.8% of the respondents supported 'setting' as a basis for provision in mathematics (Chryiwsky and Kennard 1997: 53).

In a sense the 'general versus specific' question is misleading since teachers will want to know how best to develop mathematical ability irrespective of a pupil's general profile of abilities. Having a view about the nature of mathematical ability is a key element in determining the most appropriate forms of provision for able pupils.

The characteristic abilities associated with able children of secondary school age

Summary

Krutetskii's model is employed as the basis for this summary; additional points of interpretation emphasising links with related studies are shown in italics.

Table 1.2 Characteristic abilities associated with mathematically able children of secondary school age

Grasping the formal structure of a problem in a way that leads to ideas for action. *Establishing the direction of the problem.*

Generalising from the study of examples. *Searching for and recognising pattern, exploring special cases in a systematic way leading to conjectures about possible relationships.*

Generalising approaches to problem solving.

Reasoning in a logical way and as a consequence developing chains of reasoning. *Explaining, verifying, justifying, proving.*

Using mathematical symbols as part of the thinking process. *Representing mathematical situations using algebraic notation.*

Thinking flexibly; adapting their ways of approaching problems and switching from one mode of thought to another.

Reversing their direction of thought; working forwards and backwards in an attempt to solve a problem.

Leaving out intermediate steps in a logical argument and thinking in abbreviated mathematical forms. *Taking valid shortcuts.*

Remembering generalised mathematical relationships, problem types, generalised ways of approaching problems and patterns of reasoning.

The characteristic abilities associated with able pupils of primary school age

According to Krutetskii, able pupils in the primary years have embryonic forms of some of the abilities identified above. He did not, however, attempt a strict mapping of specific abilities to specific ages and he excluded exceptionally able pupils from his study. The summary in Table 1.3 combines Krutetskii's research with elements of NNS guidance for primary teachers; as a whole it mirrors the full model for secondary age children in Table 1.2. Typically, this profile of abilities will be more representative of pupils in the later primary years but younger, exceptionally able pupils, will also exhibit some of these characteristics.

The observations reported by Straker about able pupils in the infant years follow in Table 1.4.

9

Table 1.3 Characteristic abilities associated with mathematically able children of primary school age

Grasping the formal structure of a problem.

Generalising, initially through the recognition of instances of a general rule and later from the study of examples.

Generalising approaches to problem solving.

Leaving out intermediate steps when solving familiar problems.

Thinking flexibly as a consequence of appropriate teacher intervention.

Using mathematical symbols.

Developing logical arguments.

Remembering generalised results.

Table 1.4 Characteristic abilities associated with mathematically able children in the infant years

Generalising, initially through the recognition of instances of a general rule. *Classifying and sorting; recognising numerical and geometrical patterns.*

Perceiving relationships between quantities. *Ordering objects according to size.*

Reasoning using logical connectives.

The implications of this emerging structure of abilities are explored in subsequent chapters. In particular, consideration is given to the way in which this framework can inform a general strategy for provision and the usefulness of the framework for making sense of the mathematical behaviour of able children in both the primary and secondary age phases.

Chapter 2

Mathematically able children and the National Curriculum

At the end of each attainment target in the National Curriculum for mathematics (DfEE/QCA 1999) there are statements about 'exceptional performance' that are intended to help teachers differentiate their work for very able pupils, typically in Key Stage 3, working in advance of Level 8. The statement for 'Using and applying mathematics' is:

Exceptional performance

> Pupils *give reasons* for the choices they make when *investigating* within mathematics itself or when using mathematics to *analyse* tasks; these reasons explain why particular lines of enquiry are followed and others rejected. Pupils *apply* the mathematics they know in familiar and unfamiliar contexts. Pupils *use mathematical language and symbols* effectively in presenting a *convincing reasoned argument*. Their reports include mathematical *justifications*, *explaining* their solutions to problems involving a number of features or variables.   (DfEE/QCA 1999: emphasis added)

The italicised parts of this statement are intended to emphasise processes such as reasoning, analysing, using mathematical language and symbols, convincing, justifying and explaining in the context of investigating and problem solving. This formulation of 'exceptional performance' seems to reinforce the idea that mathematically able children are expected to display mathematical behaviour characterised by processes associated with enquiry and problem solving. Other statements of exceptional performance, to be found under the remaining attainment targets, are described in terms of content-oriented facts and skills but it is clear that these content areas are intended to be the contexts for the development of processes. In a significant departure from the 1995 version of the National Curriculum for mathematics there is no separate section in the programmes of study for each Key Stage devoted to using and applying mathematics. Instead the expectations for this particular attainment target are embedded in the sections on 'Number', 'Algebra', 'Shape, space and measures' and

'Handling data'. Thus, for *each* attainment target at *all* Key Stages there are three recommended strands of development comprising *problem solving, communicating* and *reasoning*.

An obvious inference to draw from the use of the term 'exceptional performance' is that pupils working above Level 8 are 'exceptionally able'. Pupils whose performance is 'exceptional' are working far in advance of the expected attainment for the majority of pupils at Key Stage 3 and even more so if the description were to be applied to pupils in Key Stage 2. However, pupils reaching Level 8 at the end of Key Stage 3 are surely also to be thought of as 'very able', if not 'exceptional'. The same might be said of pupils reaching Level 6 at the end of Key Stage 2. It is clear, though, that this kind of approach to the identification of such pupils is based on the *extent* to which they are 'working above the expected level' for their peer group. There is a real possibility, however, that too narrow a group of pupils will be identified. In the 2000 Key Stage 3 Standard Assessment Tasks (SATs), for example, only 3% of pupils achieved Level 8 or above. A further 16% achieved Level 7. It seems appropriate to regard these pupils as very able too, but this would extend the classification of very able and exceptional pupils to around 19% of a year group. This kind of approach always leads to this kind of dilemma.

Wherever a line is drawn some pupils will be overlooked. The proportion of pupils in maintained secondary schools gaining A* and A grades in GCSE mathematics in 2000 was 9.3%. Should the term 'mathematically able' be reserved for this group? How should the 24.5% of pupils achieving a Level 5 in the 2000 Key Stage 2 national tests be regarded? After a few more years patterns may begin to emerge and some schools may wish to use these as indicative of the proportion of pupils to be classified as 'able', 'very able' or 'exceptionally able'.

The implications of a National Curriculum that has expected levels of attainment for the majority of pupils and that employs terms such as 'exceptional performance' have so far been discussed in terms of national data. The recent EiC initiative adopts a definition that is *relative* to individual schools but that still relies on the notion of pupils working at levels above those typical of their peers. It also introduces alternative terminology. The EiC initiative expects all secondary schools to:

> Identify a gifted and talented pupil cohort comprising 5–10% of pupils in each year group within Key Stages 3 and 4.

It goes on to say:

> These are pupils who achieve, or who have the ability to achieve, at a level significantly in advance of the average for *their* year group in *their* school. (DfEE 2000a: 39, emphasis added)

In a sense this initiative is telling secondary schools where to draw the line. It is also reserving the term 'gifted' for high ability in academic areas of the school curriculum such as mathematics. Such cut-off

12

figures will have to be interpreted by schools with some caution. It must be remembered, for example, that while high achievement is likely to indicate high ability, low achievement is not always an indicator of low ability. There is still a need, therefore, for a discerning classroom-based approach to identification in addition to any reliance on nationally led summative assessments.

Ability and attainment

The expression of the mathematics curriculum in terms of performance raises the question of the relationship between skills, attainment and abilities. Ability and attainment are not the same thing. Attainment is influenced by factors other than ability, including pupil attitudes, perseverance, cultural and social norms and teaching quality. The recognition of a skill, on the other hand, is often taken to be an indicator of ability. If a pupil demonstrates problem-solving skills, for example, we typically say that the pupil has the *ability* to solve problems. In recognising skills we infer abilities.

Krutetskii distinguishes between skills and abilities by characterising the former as a feature of the actions of a person and the latter as the psychological traits of the person carrying out those actions. He emphasises this distinction by saying, 'the investigation of a pupil's mathematical abilities is also an investigation of his mathematical behaviour, but from a certain standpoint' (1976: 72). This standpoint is the consideration of the psychological traits or abilities that enable the pupil to master the skills associated with the successful performance of a mathematical task.

Using and applying mathematics

Analysis of the National Curriculum for mathematics (DfEE/QCA, 1999) shows that many of the characteristic abilities discussed in Chapter 1 are reflected in the various Key Stage programmes of study and attainment target levels for 'Using and applying mathematics'. The reference to 'exceptional performance' above is one illustration of this. Two further illustrations are given in Tables 2.1 and 2.2.

Other processes referred to in Chapter 1 can be tracked through in a similar way though some problems of interpretation do arise. These process abilities are pivotal to the *making of mathematics* at a personal level and must therefore be appropriately represented in the teaching of each Key Stage.

It will be remembered that Krutetskii's model of the mathematical characteristics of able school children is essentially a problem-solving model. The process abilities discussed above are aspects of this model. Other features of his model are also reflected in the National Curriculum for mathematics. This is illustrated in Table 2.3.

The simple mapping of statements from the National Curriculum on to Krutetskii's abilities conceals a problem of interpretation since, as was reported earlier, Krutetskii did not generally observe the unaided

Table 2.1 Statements relating to 'generalising'

Key Stage	Reasoning strand of the 'Number' and 'Number and algebra' attainment target (Ma2)
1	Understand a general statement and investigate whether particular cases match it.
2	Understand and investigate general statements.
3	Explore, identify, and use pattern and symmetry in algebraic contexts, investigating whether particular cases can be generalised further . . .

Make conjectures and check them for new cases. |
| 4(Higher) | Explore, identify, and use pattern and symmetry in algebraic contexts, investigating whether particular cases can be generalised further . . . |

Table 2.2 Statements relating to 'logical reasoning'

Key Stage	Reasoning strand of the 'Number' and 'Number and algebra' attainment target (Ma2)
1	Explain their methods and reasoning when solving problems involving number and data.
2	Develop logical thinking and explain their reasoning.
3	Understand the importance of a counter-example.

Show step-by-step deduction in solving a problem; explain and justify how they arrived at a conclusion.

Distinguish between a practical demonstration and proof.

Recognise the importance of assumptions when deducing results. |
| 4(Higher) | Understand the importance of a counter-example.

Understand the difference between a practical demonstration and proof.

Show step-by-step deduction in solving a problem; derive proofs using short chains of deductive reasoning.

Recognise the significance of stating constraints and assumptions when deducing results. |

search for alternative ways of solving problems in children aged 8. The general thrust of statements related to flexible thinking, however, is consistent with Krutetskii's findings. Reversibility, the curtailment of reasoning, grasping the essence of problem and memory retention are not explicitly mentioned in the National Curriculum. The first three of these could be interpreted to be features of 'mathematical reasoning' and 'developing and using their own strategies'. Memory retention, however, is qualitatively different from the other categories, and intimately connected to the nature of children's mathematical understanding. Grasping the essence of a problem will also to some extent depend on the nature of pupils' mathematical understanding and the way previously learnt skills could be employed.

14

Table 2.3 Statements relating to problem solving

	Key Stage	Problem-solving strand of the 'Shape, space and measures' attainment target (Ma3)
Able children can think flexibly; adapt their ways of approaching problems	1	Try different approaches and find ways of overcoming difficulties when solving shape and space problems.
	2	Approach spatial problems flexibly, including trying alternative approaches to overcome difficulties.
	3	Select problem-solving strategies and resources, including information and communications technology (ICT), to use in geometrical work, and monitor their effectiveness.
	4 (Higher)	Select problem-solving strategies and resources, including ICT, to use in geometrical work, and monitor their effectiveness.
		Develop and follow alternative lines of enquiry, justifying their decisions to follow or reject particular approaches.

The programmes of study in the National Curriculum for mathematics are the basis for the mathematics 'Framework' documents used by primary and secondary teachers for long-, medium- and short-term planning. Indeed, if teachers follow the relevant Framework they effectively implement the National Curriculum for a particular Key Stage. The characteristics of mathematical ability reflected in the programmes of study and attainment targets of the National Curriculum for mathematics are also a feature of the Frameworks, but expressed in slightly different ways (Tables 2.4 and 2.5).

It must be borne in mind that the sections extracted from the National Curriculum Key Stage programmes of study and the corresponding Frameworks are intended for *most* children at a Key Stage, while Krutetskii's structure of mathematical abilities is characteristic of able children only. While the National Curriculum sets out what children should be taught, Krutetskii's research identifies the abilities typical of able children. Is a view of the characteristic abilities of able children compatible with a National Curriculum that seems to reflect this view but that applies to most pupils at a Key Stage? First, it does seem that process and problem-solving abilities constitute a view of mathematical ability that is reflected in the National Curriculum and that is consistent with the standpoint that mathematics may be seen as an activity and not just a body of knowledge. Against this background the difficulty apparent in the question can only be resolved if it is accepted that it is the extent to which able pupils display these abilities that permits them to be identified. Thus the most able are distinguishable by the strength of the aptitudes, which they display relative to their peers.

Table 2.4 Framework for teaching mathematics from Reception to Year 6 (DfEE/QCA 1999, emphasis added)

Yearly Teaching Programme	Solving problems strand
2	*Reasoning about numbers or shapes:* • *Solve* mathematical problems or puzzles, *recognise* simple *patterns* and *relationships, generalise* and *predict*. Suggest extensions by asking 'What if . . .?' or 'What could I try next?' • Investigate a *general* statement about familiar numbers or shapes by finding examples that satisfy it. • *Explain* how a problem was solved.
6	*Reasoning and generalising about numbers or shapes*: • *Explain* methods and *reasoning*. • *Solve* mathematical problems or puzzles, *recognise* and explain *patterns and relationships, generalise and predict*. Suggest extensions by asking 'What if . . .?' • Make and investigate a *general* statement about familiar numbers or shapes by finding examples that satisfy it. Develop from explaining a *generalised relationship* in words to expressing it in a formula using letters as *symbols*.

Table 2.5 Framework for teaching mathematics: Years 7–9 (DfEE 2001, emphasis added)

Yearly Teaching Programme	
9	*Using and applying mathematics to solve problems strand* • *Solve* increasingly demanding problems and evaluate solutions; explore *connections* in mathematics across a range of contexts. • Represent problems and synthesise information in algebraic, geometric or graphical form; *move from one to the other* to gain a different perspective on the problem. • Solve substantial problems by *breaking them into simpler tasks*. • Present a concise, reasoned argument, *using symbols*, diagrams, graphs and related explanatory text. • Suggest extensions to problems, *conjecture and generalise*; identify exceptional cases or counter-examples, *explaining why*. *Shape, space and measures strand* • Distinguish between conventions, definitions and *derived* properties; distinguish between practical demonstrations and *proof*; know underlying assumptions, recognise their importance and limitations and the effect of varying them.

Chapter 3

Pupils' self-perceptions

Another starting point in the discussion of ability and attainment is to ask children for their views. Over a two-year period, mathematically able Year 9 children attending a series of Royal Institution Mathematics Master Classes held at the University of Sunderland were given a questionnaire to complete. Additional questionnaires were given to pupils in schools in which case studies of able children were being undertaken (REACH Project, University of Sunderland). A total of 83 completed questionnaires revealed some fascinating points of view. Two questions in the survey are discussed below. Pupils' responses are very interesting and reveal how insightful they are when reflecting on their own abilities. The structure of abilities put forward at the end of Chapter 1 provides a useful basis for interpreting pupils' comments.

1. How can you tell you are good at mathematics?

The most frequently given responses are:

- I get high test results.
- I am in the top set.
- I find it easy to understand.
- I enjoy mathematics.
- I do not need much help.
- I was selected for the Mathematics Challenge Classes.
- My homework and class work are good.
- The teacher praises me.

Not surprisingly, most of the children give as their basis for 'knowing' that they are good at mathematics the twin reasons of high test scores and membership of the top set for mathematics. If this is how pupils 'know' they are good it is interesting to ask about the extent to which high test scores and setting are also used by teachers as a basis for identifying mathematically able children. The survey of secondary mathematics teachers referred to in Chapter 2 gives some indication that these factors are not sufficient, since only 45 per cent of the teachers felt that there was a clear method for identifying able children (Chyriwsky and Kennard 1997: 51). This issue is explored further in Chapter 4, where a case will be made for employing the structure of abilities discussed in Chapter 1. Central to this case is the notion that, the *recognition* of pupils' *abilities* is an important part of any attempt to promote and develop these same abilities.

The 'enjoyment' of mathematics figured quite highly in the list, with one pupil commenting:

> I wouldn't enjoy it if I was bad at it.

Others commented:

> I can often understand new concepts quickly and easily.

> You can tell if you are good at mathematics if you can understand things when in a maths lesson. It doesn't have to be straight away though. You can put it to good use in other situations in life, not just maths lessons.

> Because I eventually get the answer and I don't give up easily.

These comments recognise the abilities to grasp new ideas and apply mathematics (a 'mathematical cast of mind') and perseverance as characteristics of able pupils.

2. What is your method for solving a mathematical problem or following an investigation?

Some of the pupils' responses proved to be very articulate and reflect the structure of abilities discussed in Chapter 1.

- *Think flexibly, specialise*

> I try to break the investigation down first and then as I go on start building it back up. (Pupil A)

> If I can't do the problem which has been set I change it a bit so it is easier. When I work it out the easier way I then have an idea of how to complete the original problem. (Pupil B)

- *Search for and recognise pattern, generalise*

> If I have a problem I usually look for different examples and see if I can see a pattern. I then try out my theories on a new set of numbers work, and then try to find some numbers that do not, checking that my solution is correct. (Pupil C)

I look at the information I've got and try to find out any connections between it. I then try to write a rule from my findings which can be applied to any examples I come up with. Sometimes I make a table of results using my generalised principle. (Pupil D)

- *Reverse direction of thought*

  I often try to solve problems backwards i.e. find the answer and then work through the maths. (Pupil E)

- *Grasp the formal structure of a problem in a way that leads to ideas for action*

  1. Read the question two or three times over.
  2. Think of ways in which to solve it.
  3. Jot down some ideas. (Pupil F)

- *Specialise and use symbols*

  If faced with a mathematical problem I always simplify it as much as I can to start with. Then, if appropriate, I might use letters instead of numbers. (Pupil G)

- *Search for pattern, think flexibly*

  I usually just see if I can find a pattern and then work from that. If I can't find a pattern then I experiment with the information I have got and see what I can find out. (Pupil H)

- *Use and manipulate symbols*

  I use algebra quite a lot because algebra is probably the best method of studying a problem or investigation. (Pupil I)

- *Have a good memory for previously learnt material*

  I would solve a problem by first looking at my data and analysing it then work out which method would be the best to use, e.g. Pythagoras' Rule or trigonometry. I apply everything I know on the subject to help me tackle it as best I can and if I discover I don't know how, or can't do it, I ask for help. Sometimes applying my knowledge may mean conducting an experiment of some sort. (Pupil J)

- *Grasp the essence of the problem, specialise, search for pattern, generalise, test, symbolise, think flexibly.*

  First of all I write down what I am going to do or what I am trying to find out. I then start getting results for some simple examples and I put the results into a table. I write down any patterns that I find in those results. I then try to find a formula. Once I have found a formula, I test it three or four times. If my formula works, I write a conclusion including my formula in words and in algebra. If my formula does not work then I look for a new one. (Pupil K)

19

- *Think flexibly and logically*

  By 'tackle the problem' I mean that sometimes I will use trial and improvement, learning from my mistakes and trying to arrive at a logical conclusion. (Pupil L)

As has already been noted, some able pupils see themselves as persistent. Thus:

  I read it carefully a few times and try to understand the instructions or problem. Then I tackle the problem the best way I can. I try hard, but sometimes I get very frustrated. If that happens I get muddled and usually write the wrong answer down. Anyway, I try and solve it but if I cannot I ask my teacher for clues and then try to complete it myself. I think it is more rewarding if you work hard at a problem and eventually come up with the answer yourself. You feel very pleased with yourself. (Pupil M)

These illustrations of pupil self-perceptions seem to suggest that discussion *between* groups of able children about the methods that they employ could be a productive way of deepening understanding of the methods themselves. The self-awareness shown by these able pupils is consistent with research that indicates that highly able pupils generally exhibit 'self-regulation'; that is, 'they know how they learn best and can monitor their own learning' (Freeman 1998: 12).

Chapter 4

Teaching approaches that challenge mathematically able pupils

In the preceding chapters a fuller picture of the mathematical characteristics of able children has emerged. Could the profile of abilities described be of use to teachers in ordinary classrooms? If so, for what purpose? One clear purpose is to aid in the identification of able children and in this context reference has already been made to the checklist devised by Denton and Postlethwaite (1985) containing 22 items largely derived from the model of abilities put forward by Krutetskii (1976). Before reporting the outcome of their work it is worth mentioning that they had previously looked at the effectiveness of teachers' judgement compared with testing in the identification of able children. In this part of their study they gave a sample of Year 9 pupils a range of tests of general aptitudes and attitudes. The results were used to predict later exam success. Teachers were asked to make similar predictions. The teachers' predictions were based on overall judgements about ability and attainment gathered through normal weekly assessments and classroom contact. When the exam results eventually became known it was found that teachers of mathematics were as effective as the tests in predicting future performance.

Both of these approaches to the identification of able children are, however, susceptible to error. Other studies point to wide discrepancies between teachers' judgement and objective measures such as IQ tests (Freeman 1998: 8). In order to study the effectiveness of teachers' judgement more closely teachers in the Denton and Postlethwaite study were asked to use the checklist over a period of two to three weeks. This revealed that 'checklists, used over a short period in the way that is widely recommended, had done nothing to add to what teachers could achieve without them' (Denton and Postlethwaite 1985: 99). In other words, teachers were no more effective at identifying able children with the checklist than without it.

Denton and Postlethwaite followed up this initial work by asking a small group of teachers to use the checklist over a longer period of about three months. An observer was also present to help with the completion of the checklist. Although Denton and Postlethwaite felt

Identification through challenge

that the use of their checklist over this extended period was more worthwhile, the recording of observations was very time consuming. They also emphasised that another problem was the availability of checklist behaviour. The latter may be seen to be related to the nature of the tasks set to pupils as well as the forms of interaction between teachers and pupils. If able pupils are undertaking routine work in a classroom where there is little or no opportunity for discussion, it seems clear that these pupils are unlikely to exhibit checklist behaviour.

There is no mention in the study of teachers using the checklist experiencing any problems of interpretation. The items in the test were validated by testing and thus there is a sense in which their meaning must also be sought in terms of these tests. A similar point can be made about attempts to interpret Krutetskii's categories, which were based on 79 different tests! To what extent were teachers able to use the checklist items in the way that was intended? It also seems that a checklist of so many items is difficult to complete in a busy classroom.

Taking a cross-curricular view of the use of checklists, Freeman (1998) refers to work which lists ways in which very able pupils differ from their less able peers. Table 4.1 shows the general criteria, which most strongly resemble elements of Krutetskii's profile of mathematical abilities.

Table 4.1 Characteristics of very able pupils

Cross-curricular characteristics	Mathematical characteristics
Solving problems – they get to the essentials quickly	They grasp the formal structure of a problem in a way that leads to ideas for action
Flexibility – they utilise different methods when learning and solving problems and work in systematic ways	Think flexibly, adapting their ways of approaching problems and switching from one mode of thought to another
They have excellent memory and use of knowledge	They remember generalised mathematical relationships, problem types, generalised ways of approaching problems and patterns of reasoning

Other characteristics include: self-regulation or successfully guiding their own learning and problem-solving activities (see the high levels of self-awareness revealed by pupils in Chapter 3); speed of thought as a consequence of effective planning and quick decision making; preference for complexity, making games and tasks more complex as a way of sustaining interest, high task commitment; they may read, write and speak from an early age (1998: 12).

Some limitations in the sole use of National Curriculum tests or the setting of arbitrary proportions of the population for identification purposes were discussed in Chapter 2. Effective identification will draw on a range of mutually supportive evidence including reliable characterisations of mathematically able pupils. But how can these characterisations best be used? To what purpose can they be put? Is it that we simply want to be able to make ever more accurate predictions about pupils' performance? Of course that would be helpful, but there is a strong case to be made for using subject-specific characterisations of high ability to inform teaching methods and curriculum provision: that is, using the subject-specific characterisation *actively* to plan and teach able pupils and in clear contrast to the use of a checklist for identification purposes only. Given that children *are* responding to challenging material, teachers need an interpretive framework that facilitates the recognition of key abilities. It is not simply the recognition of these abilities, however, that concerns teachers. They will also be concerned to develop those same abilities through interaction and intervention. This approach, sometimes referred to as 'identification through provision', is strongly supported in a recent review of research in this field (Freeman 1998).

There are three strands to this emerging model of classroom based provision.

1. At the heart of the model is the teacher's view of the nature of mathematical ability. This constitutes an interpretive framework for making sense of pupils' mathematical abilities.
2. A teacher's interpretive framework will influence the design of an appropriately challenging curriculum.
3. A teacher's interpretive framework will influence ways of interacting with pupils, in particular the opportunities for mathematical characteristics to be recognised and promoted.

This approach *simultaneously* seeks to recognise and promote children's mathematical abilities and is summarised in Figure 4.1.

The **discerning teacher** *model of provision for mathematically able pupils*

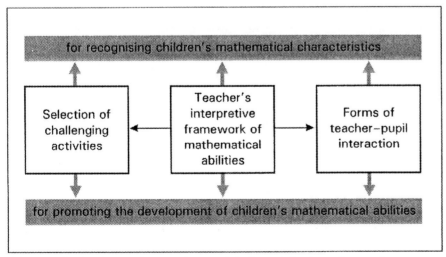

Figure 4.1 The *discerning teacher* model of provision in ordinary classrooms

23

This approach to provision is not primarily concerned with predicting future success. It focuses attention on the development of pupils' mathematical abilities and as such must be seen as continuous over time. The teachers' interpretive framework of mathematical abilities is a basis for interacting with pupils. The work of Krutetskii and others provides a useful starting point for such a framework. Over a period of time, problems of interpretation can be explored by accumulating samples of pupils' work that appear to exemplify the components of such a framework. The case studies in this book attempt to do this; further examples of pupils' work with accompanying interpretation will be published as part of the Qualifications and Curriculum Authority's (QCA's) Gifted and Talented Exemplification Project (QCA forthcoming).

Mathematical understanding

The emphasis that Krutetskii places on mathematically able pupils remembering generalised approaches resonates with other studies examining the nature of mathematical understanding. Earlier discussion focused on the notion that mathematics may be viewed as an activity and suggested that process and problem-solving abilities are pivotal to children *making* mathematics at a personal level. An approach that allows children to make mathematics at a personal level is one that provides them with opportunities to be actively reflective about their learning. This is in contrast to an approach in which children passively receive knowledge from their teachers. Skemp describes the consequence of these approaches in terms of 'relational understanding' and 'instrumental understanding' respectively (Skemp 1979: 259). With the latter approach there is a proliferation of rule learning; mathematics is learnt as a set of unconnected rules that need to be remembered. When children are actively reflecting on their work, however, they explore their own mathematical meanings and make connections with previously learnt material. The emphasis is on finding generalised approaches and relationships within the overall conceptual network.

For example, at an instrumental level children may be *given* the following rules about the areas of simple shapes:

$$\text{area of rectangle} = \text{length} \times \text{width}$$

$$\text{area of a triangle} = \tfrac{1}{2}\,\text{base} \times \text{height}$$

$$\text{area of parallelogram} = \text{base} \times \text{height}$$

and so on. When faced with a question their task is to recall the right rule for the particular shape under consideration. This approach clearly places a considerable burden on children's memory. At a relational level children will learn that in general the area of simple shapes can be found by changing them in such a way that they resemble a shape for which the area is known. For example, to find the area of a parallelogram make it look like a rectangle and to find the area of a triangle make it look like a parallelogram and reason from there (see Skemp 1979: 259 for a slightly different interpretation). When faced with a question their task is to relate it to an existing conceptual structure or 'schema'. Generalised approaches permit rules to be recreated if they are temporarily forgotten. In Skemp's terms this means that:

> there is more to learn, because higher-order concepts are involved, and more connections; but less to remember because once learnt it forms a cohesive whole, from which an indefinitely large number of particular plans can be derived.   (1979: 260)

Of course, having rules readily available is important when particular problem types are being met on a frequent basis or when faced with a test or examination. The key point about relational understanding is that previous approaches can be adapted to new mathematical situations through the independent efforts of the learner. Effective mathematics teaching will facilitate the making of links between areas of content.

Providing challenge through discussion

In order for pupils to reveal their mathematical characteristics they need to engage in challenging activities; in order for teachers to recognise and develop these abilities they need to engage in discussion with their pupils. It follows that the nature and form of oral and written communication between teachers and pupils plays a key role in these processes. From a different standpoint, the development of communicative processes is a desirable objective in its own right. Thus:

Forms of teacher–pupil interaction

> The quality of pupils' mathematical thinking as well as their ability to express themselves are considerably enhanced by discussion.   (HMI 1985: 39)

There is evidence to suggest, however, that the typical form of teacher–pupil interaction in both primary and secondary classrooms is characterised by teacher exposition. Pupil responses are typically brief (Shuard 1986: 90–93; Black and Wiliam 1998: 11). Other research shows that teachers' questions to pupils are most often aimed at testing pure recall and that pupils' responses rarely feature evaluative or reflective thought (Kerry 1981; Black and Wiliam 1998: 11). In another report the results of a questionnaire revealed that 44% of Year 7 pupils and 45% of Year 9 pupils had never spoken directly to their teachers about their work (National Commission on Education 1993: 205).

Discussion is a consequence of mutual questioning, ambiguity and attempts to convey meaning. The role of the teacher is to *initiate* dialogue. Even when a teacher is apparently responding to pupils' requests for help there is an opportunity to generate discussion. This can be achieved through forms of questioning that are supportive and encouraging and that *probe for meaning*. For example:

- Can you tell me what you've been thinking about?
- That sounds very interesting. Can you tell me a little more about . . .?
- Have you considered . . .? Would it be worthwhile thinking about that?
- You've written . . . I can't quite understand what you mean by it. Can you explain it to me please?
- How do you know your results/conclusion are right? Convince me.
- What other questions could you ask about this?

Fielker describes the teacher's role as crucial in:

> acting as a chairperson, relaying different opinions backwards and forwards, playing devil's advocate, intervening in subtle ways to ask a crucial question, introducing new ideas, influencing the direction, recalling earlier comments, comparing and contrasting, or perhaps importantly saying nothing at all. (1997: 18)

The only realistic way that teachers can create the time for sustained dialogue with pupils is to encourage pupils to become *less dependent* on themselves. This is not as strange as it first seems! Thus a class of pupils that resorts to 'hands up' at the first sign of difficulty will not permit a teacher the time to engage in protracted 'talk'. An effective alternative is to encourage pupils to discuss problems between themselves. If pupils are placed in groups for this purpose then independence can be developed over time. Useful strategies for this purpose include the following:

- When responding to a 'hand up' from a pupil in a group check first that the nature of the problem is shared by the whole group. Ask group members in turn to specify the problem to discover the extent of mutual understanding in the group. If the 'hand up' relates to an individual problem or some group members do not seem to understand why the teacher has been called over then the teacher can give the group more time and come back later. Otherwise discussion can be generated using forms of the questions above .
- When approaching a group to initiate a discussion have it in mind to check agreement among group members. Each group member can be asked to give his or her version of the thinking undertaken so far. Sources of ambiguity and disagreement can provoke further debate. The question forms mentioned above can be employed.
- All group members must listen to the comments made by their peers. All serious contributions should be valued. Sensitivity is needed to deal with the consequent emotional states of pupils,

which will vary from frustration and disappointment to elation. In the first of these it may be appropriate to ease tension by giving the pupils some information.

Pupils will become more self-reliant if teachers express genuine *interest* in pupils' ideas. Fielker argues that even if the ideas offered by pupils are wrong, what matters is that they are participating in a debate that involves 'the evaluation, the weighing up of reasons for and against given by their classmates'; as a consequence they will 'learn to listen to each other' and 'make their own judgements' (1997: 25).

Class or group introductions can begin with questions! Another useful tactic to build pupils' self-confidence is to ask them to discuss initial responses in pairs before giving the whole class feedback. Lesson summaries can contrast the methods used by different groups in approaching a problem. Any diversity of expression or methodology between pupils can provide a basis for the development of understanding through dialogue. Thus class discussion can focus on:

- common errors
- novel methods
- particular pupil expressions
- agreements and disagreements
- reports by group representatives
- misconceptions.

OFSTED reviews emphasise these points. Thus at Key Stage 2:

> In the better lessons teachers praise pupils' achievements and questioning is perceptive and challenging.   (OFSTED 1995: 11)

And at Key Stages 3 and 4:

> A feature of many good lessons, observed in Key Stage 4 particularly, was a closing class discussion in which the teacher drew together the main points of the lesson effectively, drawing on conclusions from pupils.   (OFSTED 1995: 13)

> Lessons in which there is good whole class discussion during which pupils ask questions and talk about underlying mathematical ideas and skills being taught are strongly correlated with good progress.   (OFSTED 1999b)

The National Numeracy Strategy for Key Stages 1, 2 and 3 offers guidance that reflects many of the preceding points. In particular, it recommends that teachers encourage pupils to explain their mathematical reasoning. Significantly there is an expectation that pupils are not only fluent in an 'instrumental' sense but also in a 'relational' sense too (DfEE 1999: §1, p. 1; DfEE 2001: §1). Questioning during the main part of a lesson and during the plenary part serves a variety of purposes, including motivating pupils through participation, but, importantly, it can extend pupils' mathematical abilities. If pupils are able to talk about their understanding then teachers can make judgements about how best to 'form' their future progress. As well as allowing time for pupils to think and respond teachers should not fall into the trap of readily accepting correct answers from a minority of pupils, which may allow the lesson to push ahead 'but is actually out of touch with the understanding of most of the class' (Black and Wiliam 1998: 11).

With the characteristic abilities of able children in mind the question forms above can be adapted as follows:

- Tell me in your own words what this problem is getting at.
- What patterns led you to make your generalisation?
- Tell me about the methods you used, including any that did not seem to work.
- Explain the meaning of your symbols in this problem.
- Take me through each step of your reasoning.
- What previously learnt mathematics did you find useful?
- Did you find any inverse relationships?

Challenging pupils through discussion is a way of encouraging them to think in a relational manner. The thrust of the above arguments is that pupils actively engaged in reflective discussion will reveal their mathematical abilities to a discerning teacher, who will then be able to make judgements about ways of extending or promoting these abilities still further.

Selecting challenging activities

Challenge through problem solving, enquiry and a focus on mathematical proof

A powerful way to generate discussion is through the consideration of problems or the consideration of a set of interrelated questions. The two activities are not mutually exclusive. In order to solve a problem it may be necessary to conduct an investigation and vice versa. Both activities are characterised by the opportunities that they provide for the development of process abilities. They will utilise or create a demand for facts and skills but will not usually be solely associated with the practice and rehearsal of these elements of mathematical knowledge. For mathematics teachers actively planning a distinct curriculum for the most able it is helpful to ask, 'Where is the challenge?' and to apply this question to the tasks given to pupils and to the introduction of mathematical ideas.

For example, consider the following tasks for pupils.

1. *Factual recall.* What is the formula for the area of a circle?

2. *Skill rehearsal.* Use $A = \pi r^2$ to find the area of a circle when (a) $r = 10\,cm$ (b) $r = 4\,cm$.

3. *Problem/enquiry.* A goat is put out to graze in a square field measuring $100\,m \times 100\,m$. The goat is tethered so that it can

never cross a path, which runs diagonally across the field. The farmer wants the goat to be able to graze the largest possible area. How long should the tethering rope be and at what point should the rope be fixed in order that the farmer can achieve her aim? Investigate the best way to tether the goat in fields of different shapes.

What demands do these tasks make on pupils? The first question is merely asking for the recollection of a mathematical fact. The second task requires the rehearsal of a mathematical skill. For able mathematicians the problem about the goat clearly represents more of a challenge than the more routine exercise that precedes it.

The method of introduction of this topic also provides opportunities for the teacher to stimulate curiosity and present different levels of challenge. Three possibilities for introducing the 'area of a circle' are outlined below:

1. *Definition.* In this case the teacher *gives* the formula for finding the area of a circle to the pupils. This will typically be followed by a worked example before the setting of rehearsal exercises.

2. *Problem/enquiry.* In this case the pupils are introduced to the Ahmes Papyrus, which was written about 4000 years ago (Kennard 1992: 30). Using a diagram similar to Figure 4.2 the Egyptians came up with a formula for finding the area of a circle. The pupils are asked to find this formula. One approach would be to use the area of the octagon as an approximation to the area of the circle.

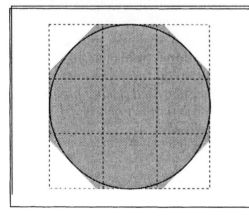

Figure 4.2 Finding the area of a circle using the area of an octagon

3. *Problem.* In this case the teacher asks the pupils to draw circles of different radii. These are subsequently cut up into sectors (say 18 in total), and rearranged to form a rectangle (Figure 4.3). The pupils are asked to interpret the lengths of the rectangle in terms of lengths of the circle and from there *develop* a formula for the area of a circle. Discussion would utilise relational understanding; in particular the generalised approach of transforming shapes whose areas are not known into shapes for which methods for finding areas already exist.

29

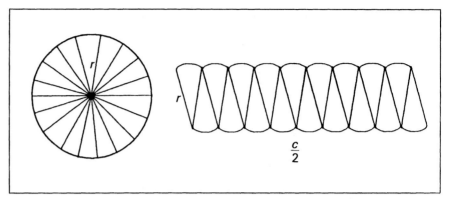

Figure 4.3 Finding the area of a circle by dividing it into sectors

Children experiencing only the teacher's definition and skills rehearsals are in a sense simply practising the teacher's examples of mathematics rather than being challenged to make mathematics at a personal level. At any Key Stage, however, pupils should experience a range of learning opportunities including problem solving and enquiry based activities (Cockcroft 1982: para. 243). It is also important that children experience success. A differentiated approach to the teaching of mathematics is one that provides *challenge with success* in order to sustain positive pupil attitudes.

The problem tasks and introductions above offer opportunities for pupils to construct chains of mathematical reasoning, which is a key feature of the model put forward by Krutetskii. Activities of this nature are also consistent with a more noticeable emphasis on proof in the revised National Curriculum (DfEE/QCA 1999) and the *Framework for Teaching Mathematics: Years 7, 8 and 9* (DfEE 2001) (see Table 2.2). In selecting activities with a focus on proof, teachers can challenge pupils to gain additional insights into the nature of mathematics itself. For example, children from a young age are asked to consider what happens when two odd numbers are added. (See, for example, the *Framework for Teaching Mathematics from Reception to Year 6*, examples for Years 4, 5 and 6 (DfEE 1999: 19)). Children will usually begin by looking at special cases:

$$3 + 3 = 6$$

$$5 + 5 = 10$$

$$7 + 7 = 14$$

After a while they will notice that all of their answers are even numbers. For the moment they are content to believe that the addition of two odd numbers always gives an even number. They rely on the experimental data, which they have generated. They cannot find any counter-examples, which would shake this belief. The result is true; it is a mathematical fact. Using a similar approach, other results are easily established for other additive combinations (e.g. even number + even number = even number). Later, further *depth* can be achieved by representing odd and even numbers in general forms using

30

symbolic notation. One way of doing this is to explore the *n*th term of a sequence of even numbers. Thus:

Position of term in sequence: 1, 2, 3, 4, 5, . . ., n

Sequence of even numbers: 2, 4, 6, 8, 10, . . ., $2n$

A general even number will therefore have the form $2n$. Alternatively, argue that an even number is always a multiple of 2, so we can think of a general even number as one made up of n multiples of 2. Since an odd number is always one more or one less than an even number a general odd number has the form $2n + 1$ or $2n - 1$. It is now possible to view the addition of two odd numbers differently.

> Let $2p + 1$ and $2q + 1$ be two different general odd numbers. Adding together two general odd numbers, that is any two odd numbers, takes the form $(2p + 1) + (2q + 1)$, which is $2p + 2q + 2$; but this is the same as $2(p + q + 1)$, which is clearly a multiple of 2. In other words, the addition of two odd numbers always results in an even number.

Note that this result is based on *reasoning* and not on experimental evidence. This sort of activity represents a challenge for more able pupils. It also develops pupils' mathematical understanding by furnishing them with insights relating to number theory and mathematical reasoning itself. Further illustrations from Year 9, Saturday morning Challenge Classes held in Sunderland are shown in Figures 4.4–4.6.

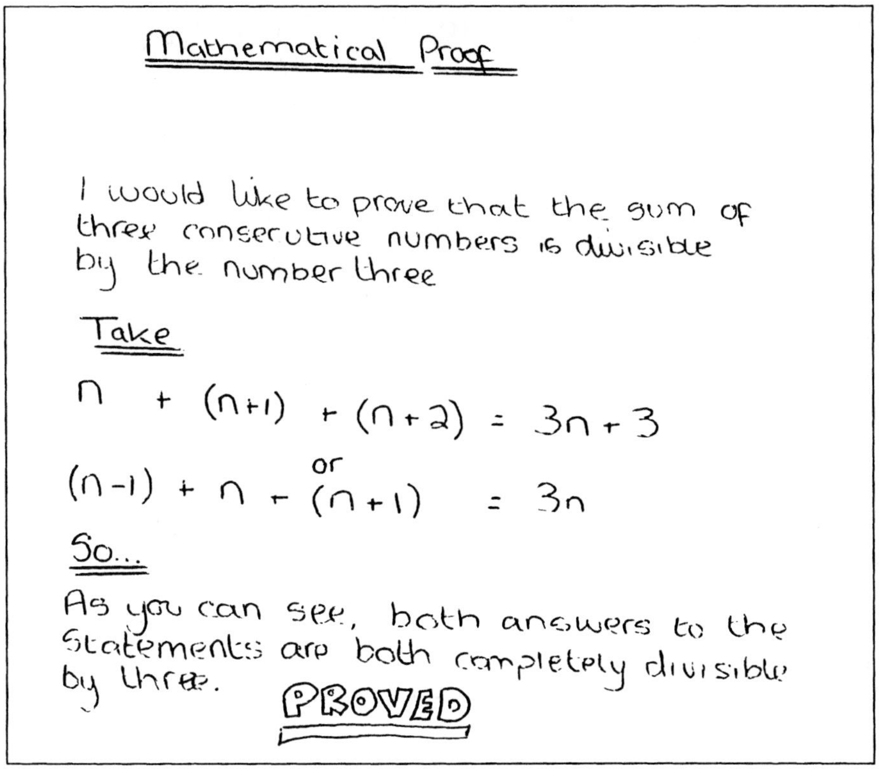

Mathematical Proof

I would like to prove that the sum of three conserutive numbers is divisible by the number three

Take

$n + (n+1) + (n+2) = 3n + 3$

or

$(n-1) + n + (n+1) = 3n$

So...

As you can see, both answers to the statements are both completely divisible by three.

PROVED

Figure 4.4 Christopher's proof

MATHEMATICAL PROOF

I want to prove that when you subtract a 3-digit number from its reverse the answer will be a multiple of 9.

Examples:

$$\begin{array}{r} 7\ 16\ 1 \\ 8\ \not{7}\ \not{2} \\ -\ 2\ 7\ 8 \\ \hline 5\ 9\ 4 = 66 \times 9 \end{array} \qquad \begin{array}{r} 8\ 17\ 1 \\ 9\ \not{8}\ \not{2} \\ -\ 2\ 8\ 9 \\ \hline 6\ 9\ 3 = 77 \times 9 \end{array}$$

Each answer is 9 multiplied by a multiple of 11, or 11 multiplied by a multiple of 9.

Formula for a general three-digit number

$$\begin{array}{r} a\ b\ c \\ c\ b\ a \\ \hline (100 \times a + 10 \times b + c) - (100 \times c + 10 \times b + a) \\ \hline \end{array}$$

$= 99a - 0b - 99c$
$= 99(a\text{-}c) = 9 \times 11(a\text{-}c)$
99 is a multiple of 9 so that means that the statement above is correct.

Figure 4.5   Karen's proof

32

I will prove that if the sum of the digits in a 3 digit number equals a number divisible by 9 then the whole number is divisible by 9.

Proof:— For a general three digit number abc.

If $\dfrac{a+b+c}{9}$ = whole number (x)

$\Rightarrow \underline{a+b+c = 9x}$

Also: abc

$= 100a + 10b + c$

$= 99a + 9b + c + a + b$

$= 99a + 9b + 9x$

$= 9(11a + b + x)$ $\qquad$ Proved!

Figure 4.6 Andrew's proof

Chapter 5

Organisational approaches for challenging mathematically able pupils

In primary or secondary school classrooms the responsibility for providing a challenging curriculum can be taken by individual teachers or by teams of teachers working together. The latter is likely to be more productive and beneficial for pupils over a period of time, especially if such provision is integrated into schemes of work or yearly teaching programmes at a particular Key Stage. The NNS, through the yearly teaching programmes for Reception to Year 9, offers teachers long-term planning schedules, which can be used to construct medium- and short-term plans.

Designing a challenging curriculum

When constructing medium-term plans, teachers will have in mind a set of minimum objectives or pupil learning outcomes that they expect most pupils to achieve. At this stage of the planning process further problems or more challenging material should be identified for the more able. In other words, problem or enquiry starting points can be selected so that able pupils achieve:

- greater depth of understanding on a current topic;
- links with previously learnt material;
- application of ideas to an unfamiliar context;
- development of process abilities;
- success and enjoyment.

These activities constitute an 'enriched' curriculum for the most able. Further 'extension' could be achieved by selecting objectives from a higher yearly teaching programme. Guidance on teaching method could also be incorporated into the medium-term plan. A possible planning format, which has the potential to pick up on these points, is shown in Table 5.1; it utilises the example on area discussed in Chapter 4.

Planning to challenge

Table 5.1 Medium-term planning for Year 9

Topic	Hours	Teaching objectives
Shape, space and measures	3	• Know and use the formula for the circumference and area of a circle • *Enrichment objective*: Find a formula for the approximate area of a circle using a diagram from the Ahmes Papyrus as a starting point • *Extension objective (Year 10, Key Stage 4 (Higher))*: Calculate areas of sectors of circles

Introduction (enrichment)

Using a diagram similar to the one shown here the Egyptians came up with a formula for finding the area of a circle. Ask pupils to find this formula.

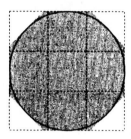

One approach would be to use the area of the octagon as an approximation to the area of the circle.

This gives $A = \frac{7}{9}d^2$.

Develop the formula by first asking pupils to draw circles of different radii. Cut these up into sectors (say 18 in total), and rearrange the sectors to form a rectangle. Interpret the lengths of the rectangle in terms of the radius and circumference of the circle, and from there deduce the formula. Equate it to Egyptian formula and come up with the Egyptian approximation to π.

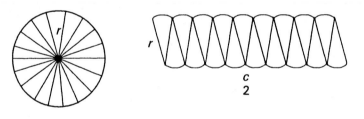

Pupil tasks

Rehearse use of the formula followed by problems.

Example:

A goat is put out to graze in a square field measuring 100m × 100m. The goat is tethered so that it can never cross a path that runs diagonally across the field. The farmer wants the goat to be able to graze the largest possible area. How long should the tethering rope be and at what point should the rope be fixed in order that the farmer can achieve her aim? Investigate the best way to tether the goat in fields of different shapes.

See also DfEE (2001: 19, 237).

Extension

See Year 9 objectives for able pupils and examples for Years 7–9 (DfEE 2001: 237).

Teachers will need to ask of their medium-term planning, 'Are the presentation of mathematical ideas and the tasks set for pupils sufficiently challenging?' Different schools will arrive at different answers, but in all schools the relevant NNS Framework will provide an invaluable starting point. This approach to curriculum planning does not require able pupils to do every routine exercise before moving on to the planned 'enrichment' or 'extension' material. If this happened it would clearly overload the pupils concerned; it therefore seems appropriate to view this material as replacing needlessly repetitive exercises. Some of the issues surrounding the merits of 'enrichment' and 'extension by drawing on the work normally designated for older year groups' is discussed later in this chapter. Further examples of this approach can be found in *Mathematical Challenges for Able Pupils in Key Stages 1 and 2* (DfEE 2000b): there is a Year 2 example on page 6 and a Year 6 example on page 7. Both of these examples, however, restrict themselves to setting out objectives without reference to guidance on teaching methods. A different example, along the lines of the Year 9 topic plan above, is shown in Table 5.2.

Table 5.2   Medium-term planning for Year 5

Topic	Hours	Teaching objectives
Numbers and the number system Properties of numbers and number sequences	1–2	• Find all the pairs of factors of any number up to 100 • *Enrichment objective*: Develop a general shorthand method for finding the factors of any number utilising the notion of square roots • *Extension objective (Year 6):* Factorise numbers to 100 into prime factors

Introduction (enrichment)

Confirm meaning: in a product like 2×7, each number is called a *factor* of 14.

If pupils work systematically they will soon notice that some products give factors that are repetitions of those found earlier. For example:

$1 \times 12 = 12$	$7 \times ?$
$2 \times 6 = 12$	$8 \times ?$
$3 \times 4 = 12$	$9 \times ?$
$4 \times 3 = 12$	$10 \times ?$
$5 \times ?$	$11 \times ?$
$6 \times 2 = 12$	$12 \times 1 = 12$

In searching for factors, how can we avoid repetitions? Elicit initial conjectures. For example: stop when we are halfway; investigate 'square numbers' first; look for a connection between where the list stops and the square root of the 'square number'; generalise.

Extension

See DfEE (2001: 21).

Chapter 8 offers a closer look at how a group of pupils responded to the challenge in Table 5.2. Their responses are interpreted in terms of the structure of mathematical abilities discussed in Chapter 1.

Medium-term plans can also be used to guide teachers towards important links between areas of content, and thus lead pupils towards a relational understanding of mathematics (see Table 5.3).

Table 5.3 Medium-term planning for Year 10 (Key Stage 4 Higher)

Topic	Hours	Teaching objectives
Geometrical reasoning: properties of triangles and other rectilinear shapes	5–6	• Recall and use trigonmetrical relationships in right-angled triangles, and use these to solve problems • *Enrichment links:* ratio, similarity and enlargement, change the subject of a formula

Links to previously learnt material

Ratios compare like quantities. For example, in these similar triangles the ratio of corresponding sides is constant:

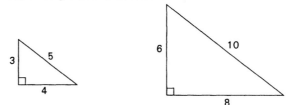

One of this pair of similar triangles is an enlargement of the other:

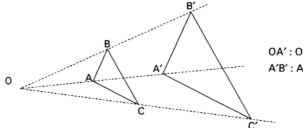

$$OA' : OA = OB' : OB = OC' : OC$$
$$A'B' : AB = A'C' : AC = B'C' : BC$$

Introduce sine θ and cosine θ as *labels* for the lengths of the sides in the right-angled triangle with a hypotenuse of 1. Use properties of enlargement to form equations connecting corresponding sides, given that one of this pair of triangles is an enlargement of the other with a scale factor of enlargement of H:

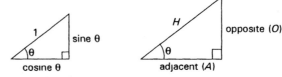

Rearrange to establish trigonometric relationships:

$$A = H\cos\theta \quad \Rightarrow \quad \cos\theta = \frac{A}{H} \qquad\qquad O = H\sin\theta \quad \Rightarrow \quad \sin\theta = \frac{O}{H}$$

Future link

Investigate how sine θ and cosine θ vary as θ varies.

The approach to establishing trigonometric relationships shown in Table 5.3 can also be used to develop the tangent ratio by adapting the initial triangle so that the adjacent side to θ is of unit length. Such an approach is in stark contrast to one that presents pupils with definitions followed by a mnemonic. The triangle shown in Figure 5.1 is typical of a mnemonic based approach.

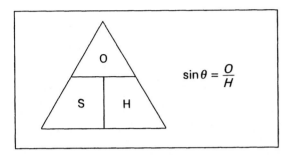

$$\sin \theta = \frac{O}{H}$$

Figure 5.1 Mnemonic based approach to learning trigonometric relationships

The aim of the approach to medium-term planning represented in Tables 5.1–5.3 is to ensure that able pupils follow a suitably differentiated programme. The additional guidance will assist teachers of setted classes or mixed ability classes to provide the challenge required in the main teaching part of a structured mathematics lesson as advised by the National Numeracy Strategy.

Published schemes

Commercially available schemes comprising lesson plans, photocopiable worksheets, textbooks and software are widely available. The key questions for teachers considering using such schemes are:

- Are the teaching objectives sufficiently explicit? Are the teaching objectives in line with the yearly teaching programmes from Reception to Year 9, or GCSE and A-level programmes?
- Are the pupils' tasks of the right standard? Are they in line with the examples in the NNS Frameworks or the demands of GCSE and A-level exam papers?
- Where is the challenge in the way mathematical ideas are presented? Are the scheme materials essentially didactic in nature? Are discussion activities identified?
- Where is the challenge in the tasks set to pupils? How often do pupils have the opportunity to tackle problems or to engage in enquiry? Are there opportunities for pupils to develop process abilities consistent with the structure of mathematical abilities represented in Tables 1.2–1.4.
- Will able pupils simply progress, albeit quickly, to the next task, chapter or worksheet without being stretched intellectually?
- Are able pupils expected to work alone for most of the time? In what circumstances do pupils have the chance to engage in protracted mathematical discussion?

39

• To what extent does the scheme support the delivery of a structured mathematics lesson?

These are not easy questions for individual teachers to consider. A collective response from all the staff in a primary school or secondary mathematics department is probably more appropriate. Nonetheless, individual teachers using such schemes on a daily basis can explore their own responses to these questions.

Puzzle and problem displays

There will typically be occasions when pupils come to individual teachers' attention because they find the work too easy, finish it too quickly or both. There may be reasons why it is not convenient to move the pupil on to the next task. For example, a workbook or work card may already be in use or a class introduction may be planned. It may also be appropriate to vary the pupil's learning experience, for example to balance the acquisition of content with the development of process abilities. On these occasions it is helpful to have a collection of puzzles and problems freely available. An effective way of making the puzzles and problems accessible is to mount them on a notice board. Pupils can then be referred to these. Solutions can be placed in files for pupils to consult, but some dialogue utilising the question forms of the previous chapter remains essential. Since the puzzles and problems are always visible they can serve to arouse interest to the point where children ask to have time to tackle them. If wall space is scarce a useful alternative is to mount the puzzles and problems on card and then place them in a box on a work surface.

Leading the provision of challenge

There is clearly much that individual teachers can do in their own classrooms to provide able children with a challenging curriculum. However, when a collective approach to the needs of able children is pursued there is evidence to suggest that this is followed by 'a general increase in the level of expectation for all pupils and this was sometimes reflected in examination results' (HMI 1992: viii). In terms of a whole-school or departmental response to the provision of challenge it is important that a lead is given by the head teacher, but substantial initiatives must come from the primary mathematics coordinator or the secondary head of department. Further support or guidance may be available from EiC 'gifted and talented' coordinators. Some useful initiatives are described opposite.

Designate a teacher to coordinate provision for able pupils

The responsibilities of the teacher would comprise:

- leading the development, implementation, monitoring and evaluation of any special provision, especially the use of an interpretive framework for promoting and developing mathematical ability;
- mutually supportive forms of identification, including testing and 'identification through challenge';
- producing medium-term planning guidance and explicating effective forms of teacher–pupil interaction.

The coordinator might also be expected to:

- liaise with other phases to help ensure progression;
- adapt the school's assessment and recording policy to take account of this special group;
- liaise with senior managers and other specialists.

Regular review meetings

These could be scheduled at half-termly or termly intervals to:

- discuss characteristics of mathematical ability;
- discuss the appropriateness of medium-term planning;
- discuss pupils' work that exemplifies mathematical ability;
- review teaching approaches aimed at generating mathematical discussion;
- review any special provision required for exceptionally able children.

It is only through regular reviews of this kind that 'policy' with respect to able children becomes meaningful, that is, it makes a difference to what teachers actually do.

Co-teaching

It is possible in most schools to arrange a programme that enables teachers to collaborate with colleagues with respect to teaching and learning approaches. In the long term, cover for short periods, even if this is only for an hour, can be achieved in primary schools with the support of the head teacher and in secondary schools through the judicious use of 'non-teaching periods'. In this context teachers can jointly look for evidence of high ability and effective forms of teacher–pupil interaction and test new materials.

Extra challenge

A further initiative centres on the enlivenment of the regular curriculum. Some possibilities are listed here.

A mathematics club

Recreational mathematics is often a source of great pleasure to schoolchildren. Puzzles and mathematical games abound and can provide many children with a focus for challenge. Clubs can run at lunchtimes and be supervised by a rota of staff, senior pupils and/or parents. An excellent website to support the running of a school mathematics club is:

http://nrich.maths.org.uk (accessed July 2001)

For secondary schools the Mathematical Association publishes a 'Secondary Maths Club Pack'.

Mathematics and logic festival

The festival can be a two- to three-week period when pupils are given a booklet of activities to pursue instead of normal homework. Some lesson time can also be given over to this project to give it added impetus. Pupils hand in their work for marking in the usual way with some pupils selected out for commendations or prizes. If pupils are encouraged to present their work attractively there will also be an opportunity to mount wall displays.

Competitions

These are sometimes managed by local education authorities or local universities. National competitions are organised by:

United Kingdom Mathematics Trust
(University of Leeds, Tel. 01132 332339)

Masterclasses

The Royal Institution of Great Britain has sponsored the growth of a nationwide programme of classes specifically intended to stimulate the interest of able schoolchildren. They are often coordinated locally by universities and local education authorities and typically run over several Saturday mornings. For further information contact:

The Royal Institution of Great Britain
www.ri.ac.uk (accessed July 2001)

Masterclasses are also supported by:

Gabbitas Truman and Thring Educational Trust
www.masterclass.co.uk (accessed July 2001)

Industry links

These are another source of potential challenge for able children. Contexts for mathematical problems can be developed in collaboration with local industrialists. For example, the University of Sunderland and Nissan Motor Manufacturing (UK) devised a mathematical challenge that focused on the steel coils used in the 'pressing' of body components. An excellent report by one of the Year 9 pupils involved can be found in Chapter 7.

Mathematical quiz

Inter-class or form quiz competitions in which the questions are about mathematics can be run at lunchtimes. They can be organised on a knockout basis in the manner of sporting competitions. Although questions will typically be presented in an oral fashion they could be combined with overhead projector slides, videotapes or other visual aids.

Mathematics magazine

With most schools having access to word processing technology it is now possible to produce a mathematics magazine that poses problems and puzzles. This might be a largely pupil-run project with some supervision from staff, senior pupils or parents. Some way of providing solutions needs to be worked out. These can appear in subsequent issues or be distributed on request. Alternatively, use the pupil magazines *Symmetry Plus* and *Mathematical Pie* published by the Mathematical Association.

Assessment and testing information

Look for World Class Tests for 9- and 13-year-olds and Advanced Extension Awards for 18-year-olds at:

www.qca.org.uk (accessed July 2001)

Acceleration, enrichment and extension

There has been vigorous debate in recent years about the most appropriate forms of overall provision for able children. Centre stage is the issue of whether it is better to accelerate able children through the designated curriculum or whether it is more appropriate to enrich and extend their experience within its normal pacing.

Acceleration typically refers to an approach that gives children access to curriculum content ahead of their years. Children 'jump' years or are 'fast tracked' through the curriculum. For example, the practice in some secondary mathematics departments has been to enter children a year early for the GCSE mathematics examination. It is comparatively rare in this country, however, for schools to move individual pupils into an older age group (HMI 1992: 14). For a secondary mathematics department with a sufficiently large group of pupils it is relatively straightforward to arrange for early entry to GCSE mathematics. It is rather more difficult to match timetables for different year groups in order for pupils to move up a year. Primary schools will not encounter the same organisational constraints in this last respect. Other questions loom large, however, about the practice of accelerating pupils in these ways.

Are secondary pupils who take their exams early obtaining A or A* grades? Is there any point in accelerating them to lower grades? How well has the mathematics been understood? Would it be more appropriate to enrich the mathematics curriculum? In their survey of secondary teachers of mathematics, Chyriwsky and Kennard found that 48% of their respondents agreed that early entry to GCSE was an appropriate strategy for dealing with able children but only 16% supported the policy of moving children up a year. However, just over 95% of the mathematics teachers agreed that enrichment was also an appropriate strategy (Chyriwsky and Kennard 1997). If pupils are moved up a year, will they experience any social or emotional drawbacks? After many years of research there is still some dispute on this question. A major research study in Australia emphatically argues that there is no evidence to suggest that children on accelerative programs suffer emotional or social damage. In fact, it argues the opposite case. That is, *exceptionally gifted children* will suffer emotional and social damage if they are not accelerated (Gross 1993: 277). On the other hand, work in the UK suggests that unless *gifted* children are already mature for their years, 'acceleration is probably not the best option' (Freeman 1991: 214).

In a broad survey of work undertaken on the acceleration of gifted children, Jones and Southern (1991) argue that there is no conclusive evidence about the emotional and social consequences of accelerating gifted children. Indeed, they point out that there are methodological problems in trying to resolve the problem since it is difficult to set up control groups; once gifted pupils have been identified it is ethically wrong to ignore them (Jones and Southern 1991: 223). However, they do claim that gifted children benefit academically from this form of provision and that in practical terms it is the only way to cope with children who can learn so quickly. An example of this is provided by an American study, which identified the top 1% of mathematically able pupils in the lower secondary years and then offered them a 'summer camp' programme. In this programme the typical pupil covered two years of schoolwork in just three weeks (Stanley 1990: 217). However, Freeman raises doubts about the generalisability of such studies by suggesting that such gains are only possible because the American system is 'slower and less differentiated than that in Europe' (Freeman 1998: 38). Her review of international research also identifies many other methodological problems in research of this kind. She found evidence that in circumstances where acceleration is the only provision possible, it can be beneficial to pupils provided sufficient care is taken to ensure adequate emotional and intellectual support for the children concerned. In the round, however, her review doubted the long-term benefits of acceleration, pointing to a study showing no significant differences in academic performance between accelerated and non-accelerated pupils once they had reached the age of 23.

Simply moving a pupil up a year may not present him or her with additional intellectual challenge in terms of cognitive skills. In other words, it is possible that the pupil is *easily* acquiring content and that challenge in terms of problem solving or mathematical discussion is still absent. If a school, in collaboration with parents, does decide to move a pupil out of his or her normal year group then it may be helpful to designate a member of staff to act as a 'mentor' to the pupil concerned. The role of the mentor would be to monitor the pupil's adjustment to change and the level and nature of the additional challenge provided. Regular reviews of progress would be very desirable in these circumstances and as a general guide the younger the pupil the more frequent these should be. This idea could be extended to involve subject mentors from outside the school in cases where a child is outstripping what the school can reasonably provide itself. For example, a primary school may obtain support from a local secondary school, and a secondary school may be able to enrol the help of a local college or university tutor.

What are the organisational implications of pupils finishing the normal curriculum early? If an individual pupil or a class of pupils completes the work in a Key Stage one or two years early, then what? Is there something suitable for them to go on to? Who will teach them? The nature of a school's responses to these questions will influence the extent to which it accelerates pupils. A recent report by the UK Mathematics Foundation is strongly critical of acceleration as a strategy and makes a strong alternative case for enrichment as the most suitable way to provide for very able pupils. It argues for an enrichment approach that expects pupils to have a 'greater depth of understanding' as well as a 'higher level of technique' in the designated yearly teaching programme, and related material that does not draw on work from later years (UK Mathematics Foundation 2000: 12). Such an approach would assist progression between year groups but makes significant demands on teachers to devise an appropriate enrichment programme. But is it realistic to expect that pupils will never encroach at all on the work of later years? Pupils will anticipate such work through the questions they ask and the work will therefore arise naturally. However, it is a vital prerequisite of the introduction of 'accelerated' material that pupils have a relational understanding of the mathematics that they have been taught and that they can confidently articulate their mathematical reasoning.

The mathematical experience of able pupils can be enriched and extended through problem-solving and enquiry approaches that emphasise mathematical discussion. This experience will be greatly enhanced when teachers employ an interpretive framework that simultaneously helps them to recognise and promote the mathematical characteristics of their children.

Grouping

In Chapter 1 it was reported that a large majority of secondary mathematics teachers favoured 'setting' as a form of pupil grouping appropriate for meeting the needs of able pupils. Setting is also favoured by some primary schools. In many other primary schools each year group is of mixed ability but children will be grouped by ability during the daily mathematics lesson. Is one method of grouping better than another? A recent review of research concluded that setting or streaming have no significant benefits for pupils' performance (Sukhnandan 1998). However, in an earlier report, HMI doubted that any one method was 'uniquely suited to the needs of the very able' (HMI 1992: 13). HMI went on to say that, 'The matching of work to the ability of the very able pupils bore little relation to the type of organisation adopted and in many classes the lack of differentiation was a distinct feature'.

The key to provision for able children is 'challenge' and grouping *per se* does not guarantee this. In keeping with other findings on the subject of grouping it seems that the beliefs and actions of teachers have a very important role to play in determining the *actual* level of challenge offered to able pupils.

Chapter 6

Case study 1: Working with able Year 9 pupils

Introduction

In the case study synopsis that follows, the mathematical task set was designed to challenge pupils within the context of their current scheme of work. The teacher-researcher (so called because the pupils are being taught as well as observed – not simply being tested), uses a questioning approach, which serves to facilitate learning *and* to reveal aspects of pupils' mathematical approaches and understanding. Occasionally pupils are asked to summarise their thinking as a check on both of these points. Although on this occasion no attempt was made to record the discussion between pupils themselves it is clearly a further source of data about their mathematical characteristics. The interpretation of the pupils' responses is interwoven in the text and makes use of Krutetskii's categories where appropriate.

Case study synopsis

General context

The case study was undertaken in a comprehensive school situated in a largely urban environment: a non-selective, mixed gender school for pupils aged 11–18, with approximately 1200 pupils on roll.

Specific context

The teacher-researcher was working with a group of four Year 9 pupils (13–14 years old). The remainder of the class were being taught by their regular class teacher. The topic in the school scheme of work was 'angles in polygons'. The group of four pupils had already learnt how to find the interior angle of a regular polygon. The extension activity was to devise a test to decide whether or not a shape tessel–lates. Time intervals are not generally indicated. Overall, the pupils spent approximately 70 minutes with the teacher-researcher.

In what follows the teacher-researcher's comments are preceded by a T. The pupils' comments are preceded by their names: Michael, Laura, Keith and Amy. Other comments are in italics and, specifically, any interpretation of mathematical abilities is shown in bold italics. Pupils' writing is shown in a handwriting font.

T: Today we are going to think about why shapes tessellate. What do I mean by tessellate?

Michael: Fit together.

T: Let's explore what we mean by 'fit together'. We've got a box of shapes here . . . so, Laura, can you pick out some shapes which fit together? We have to find out what Michael has in mind.

Laura takes some decagons and pauses.

T: What's your instinct about this shape? Will it fit together?

Michael: It won't tessellate.

Keith: No, it won't.

T: How can you be sure?

Amy: Try it.

Laura moves the decagons around provoking further comment from Michael.

Michael: There's a gap in between them . . . it's got too many sides.

T: Try some more shapes.

Michael picks up some squares, Laura some right-angled isosceles triangles, Amy some rectangles and Keith some pentagons.

T: What I'm interested in, Michael, is . . . how many shapes do you need to put down on the table before you know?

Michael puts down four squares.

T: Do you need any more?

Michael: No.

T: How sure are you about that?

Michael: Pretty sure because there are no gaps between them.

Laura and Amy agree that four shapes were sufficient for them to see that the shapes tessellated. Keith, however, has placed three pentagons together and the pupils are all agreed that a fourth would not fit into the gap.

T: OK. Write a summary of where we have got to so far.

Laura wrote:

> We are trying to find out which shapes tessellate and how you can see whether they do or not. One way of doing this is to fit them together and see if any gaps are left; if there are gaps they don't tessellate. We have noticed that right-angled isosceles triangles tessellate, squares tessellate, rectangles tessellate.

Laura's write-up reveals that she has grasped the essence of the problem. Her write-up was typical for the group. Taken with the preceding dialogue, it shows that the pupils understand that moving shapes around in order to see if they fit together without leaving any gaps is a practical way of testing whether or not shapes tessellate.

T: So far we've got a practical test. Let's work towards a test to use if we have not got any shapes around. Any ideas?

Michael: Measure the angles to see which angles fit together.

Laura: Measure the angles . . . if two angles fit together to make a straight line or 180 degrees . . . they will probably fit together.

T: What do you think, Amy? Worth exploring? Keith?

Both pupils indicate their agreement.

T: OK. Follow up your ideas.

A few minutes later Laura and Amy are looking at four quadrants of a circle joined together as one complete circle.

T: What have you got there?

Laura: They fit together to make a straight line . . . but they don't tessellate.

T: Show me.

More circles are added to reveal the gaps.

Laura: It doesn't work.

T: Try a different idea.

Laura and Amy have put forward a conjecture and set out to test it. After a while they find a counter-example, which leads them to reject their initial idea. They have disproved their conjecture by counter-example. *It seems that they were influenced by their early experience of working with rectangles and right-angled isosceles triangles. In both cases four right angles at a point fit together without leaving a gap!* **They further show a flexibility of thought in their willingness to try a new approach.**

At this point attention is switched to the two boys who are working with a set of hexagons.

T: What have you come up with Keith?

Keith: If you can divide into 360 degrees they'll be able to join ... three angles makes 360 ... that angle is 120 degrees and that will divide into 360 three times, so they fit together. [*Pointing next to a pentagon.*] This one's a pentagon ... this angle measures 110 degrees, which won't divide into 360 degrees.

T: Sounds quite promising.

Michael: We just need to know the angle ... divide it into 360 degrees to see if it fits exactly, without a decimal left over.

T: Write another summary. Summarise where you've got to.

Keith wrote:

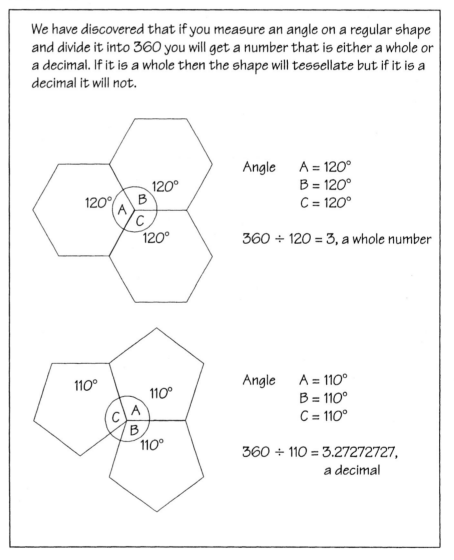

We have discovered that if you measure an angle on a regular shape and divide it into 360 you will get a number that is either a whole or a decimal. If it is a whole then the shape will tessellate but if it is a decimal it will not.

Angle A = 120°
B = 120°
C = 120°

360 ÷ 120 = 3, a whole number

Angle A = 110°
B = 110°
C = 110°

360 ÷ 110 = 3.27272727, a decimal

The pupils have put together a chain of reasoning that allows them to formulate a generalisation. At this stage, Keith is still talking about measuring the interior angle of the polygon. He was not observed doing this!

At this point attention switches back to the two girls who are looking at a set of equilateral triangles.

T: How are things developing?

Laura: Six equilateral triangles at a point add up to 360 degrees.

Amy: Angles in the middle add up to 360 degrees when they are put together. You can work out the size of the interior angle by dividing 360 degrees by six.

T: There's a clue in what you say. If we want to know if a particular shape tessellates . . . but we haven't got any to move around . . . How can we decide? Say you know the interior angle . . . Can you see a connection with what you have just done?

Laura: It goes into 360 degrees . . . it tessellates.

T: Yes. Can you see it's the same idea . . . just working in different directions?

The pupils are comfortable with this and go on to do their own write-up, which is similar to Keith's work opposite.

The pupils have reversed their reasoning. Arguing that a shape tessellates if the interior angle of a polygon is a divisor of 360 degrees is the converse of arguing that for shapes that tessellate, the interior angle is given by dividing 360 by the number of shapes at a point.

T: You seem to have a strong theory. How could you check it's true?

Michael: You could predict for a shape you hadn't tried.

T: Try that and then write it up.

*Michael and Keith choose a 15-sided polygon; Laura and Amy try an 11-sided polygon. Both pairs are able to utilise the formula they had previously learnt for finding the interior angle of a regular polygon. At one point Michael and Keith falter briefly and as a test divide 360 by the number of sides of a polygon rather than the interior angle. **They quickly spot their error.***

Michael wrote:

To test our theory we needed to predict a shape we had not tried. We chose a 15 sided shape. We needed to find its interior angle. The formula to find its total angle is $180(n-2)$. We did $180 \times 13 = 2340$. Then to find its interior angle we needed to divide 2340 by 15. The answer was $156°$. To find if this shape would tessellate we needed to find out if 156 went into $360°$. We did this by $360 \div 156 = 2.3076923$. So it does not tessellate because it did not go exactly into 360.

51

The pupils are using their generalisation to decide whether or not shapes 'not on the table' will tessellate. The pupils were convinced that these particular shapes would not tessellate despite the fact that there were no shapes of this kind to do a practical test with. Their conviction was rooted in their reasoning.

At the end of the lesson they are set the homework task of trying to express their tessellation test as a formula. Michael comes back the following week with:

$$\frac{360}{\left(\dfrac{180(n-2)}{n}\right)}$$

None of the other pupils has this expression in its entirety.

T: Let's check that the formula fits the description we've got. Keith, read out Michael's description for finding the interior angle.

Keith read from Michael's description above.

T: Amy, where in the formula has he done this?

Amy: In the brackets . . . under the line.

Keith then reads out the rest of Michael's description.

T: Laura, where does this happen?

Laura: Divide the interior angle into the 360 degrees.

Michael has expressed his awareness in mathematical symbols. The expression is still strongly related to the geometrical context.

T: Good. Now . . . can you simplify the formula? That is to say . . . make it into something that is equivalent . . . but not so complicated to look at?

There is no response from the pupils.

T: I'll make a suggestion . . . Basically what you've got is something of the form $a/\frac{b}{c}$, in other words something of the form $p\ q$ . . . a fraction . . . something over something, but the something on the bottom is a fraction. Try out this idea.

The pupils have seen the similarity in structure and after a short discussion are able to manipulate Michael's expression. With relatively little in the way of revision the pupils have remembered previously learnt skills. They are able to manipulate the symbolic expression brought in by Michael.

Michael wrote:

> To simplify this formula we used the idea of dividing a whole number by a fraction. With this we got to
>
> $$360 \times \frac{n}{180(n-2)}$$
>
> But that formula was still complicated and so we tried to divide the top and bottom by 180. The simplified formula was:
>
> $$\frac{2n}{n-2}$$
>
> The formula we got was a lot simpler than the complicated first one.

Once again the test is expressed in symbolic form, but this time it is simpler or more abbreviated. The link with the geometrical context is no longer obvious.

At this point the pupils return to the same work as the rest of the class.

Conclusion

In a case study approach the context for the interpretation of children's mathematical characteristics is clear. The use of Krutetskii's categories has meaning in terms of this classroom based context. The form of teacher–pupil interaction and the nature of the challenge provided is also available for scrutiny. Sufficient material of this nature could provide teachers with a means to be *discerning* in their own classrooms.

This case study is an extract from a paper entitled 'Providing for mathematically able children in ordinary classrooms', which was first presented at the 11th World Conference on Gifted and Talented Children, Hong Kong (1995).

Chapter 7

Case study 2: Industry links

Opportunities for challenging mathematical activities can often be found in local industries. If a sympathetic local employer can be found then consideration can be given to the selection of a task at the appropriate level of challenge. Initially it helps if the employer can offer instances of the use of mathematics. Negotiation and teacher judgement are then required to find a suitable activity. The problem described below was identified in this way and relates to car manufacturing at Nissan's plant in Sunderland. It represents a possible enrichment activity for the Year 8 key objective, 'Know and use the formula for the circumference of a circle . . .' (DfEE 2001: 11). The account is given by a Year 9 pupil attending one of the Royal Institution Mathematics Master Classes run by the University of Sunderland and Sunderland local education authority.

Introduction

Steel Coils - A Mathematical Problem

There are a lot of companies around, and quite a few make cars. If you peel the paint back from the average car, you'll see that the body is made of steel. Taking it back to the factory, that steel has been painted, rust-proofed, cut and pressed. The problem is this: the steel comes in coils, and the only information you get is the weight and the thickness.

That doesn't seem much of a problem until you have to find out the length. Productivity is going to be seriously affected if you run out of steel before the next lot arrives. Well, the weight isn't much use for finding the length, so that just leaves the thickness. If you combine that with the full diameter of the roll and the inner diameter (that bit in the middle which is left so that the coils can be put on a spindle), both of which can be measured easily, you get an equation which determines the length. Eureka! But how?

If you view the roll as a number of concentric circles, as shown in the diagram, it makes it far simpler. All right, it isn't entirely accurate, because it looks like a spiral really, but the small difference doesn't really matter.

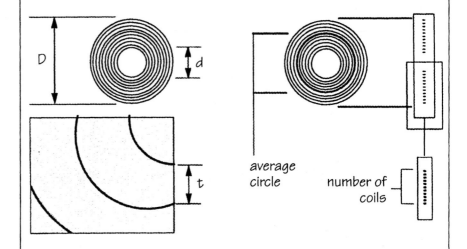

average circle

number of coils

Now what you could do is take away the middle part (the bit that rests on the spindle) from the full coil in the equation so that you've got the circles of steel left. If you then divide the remaining diameter by double the thickness you get the number of circles. This is shown as:

(In the following equations I've substituted 'D' for the full, or outer diameter, 'd' for the inner diameter and 't' represents thickness.)

$$\text{Number of circles} = \frac{D - d}{2t}$$

Why double the thickness? Well, it's just another way of halving the diameters, and you need to do that to get the correct number of coils, as the diagram illustrates.

Although you could calculate the circumference of each and every circle by adding twice the thickness to the diameter each time until you've done all of them, that's a very long way to go about it. Finding the circumference of the average circle, i.e. the one lying right between the largest and smallest circles (taken from the full and inner diameters), and then multiplying that by the number of circles is a far quicker and easier way. It's done like this:

$$\text{Circumference of the average circle} = \frac{\pi D + \pi d}{2}$$

The full equation is therefore the circumference of the average circle multiplied by the number of circles, and it looks like this:

$$\text{Total length of roll} = \frac{\pi D + \pi d}{2} \times \frac{D - d}{2t}$$

After multiplying and simplifying it a bit we get:

$$\text{Total length} = \frac{\pi}{4t}(D + d)(D - d)$$

When the bracketed part is simplified further, we finally see this:

$$\text{Total length} = \frac{\pi}{4t}\left(D^2 - d^2\right)$$

And that's it!

(Steven)

Interpretation

This is a powerful account that stretched the pupil in question. All the key insights stemmed from Steven and the group of pupils working with him. In *simplifying* the task to a set of concentric circles he has *modelled* or *grasped the essence of the problem*. Previous knowledge about averages has been *remembered*, but in a way that reveals an *appreciation of structure* or a *generalised approach*. Good *use of symbols* and *algebraic manipulation* led to the formula or *generalised result* used on the shop floor. An alternative method is described but rejected in favour of a more economical or elegant solution revealing *flexibility* of thought.

Chapter 8

Case study 3: Working with able Year 6 pupils

In a similar way to the case study reported in Chapter 6, the mathematical activity chosen was designed to challenge pupils within the context of their current mathematical topic. Once again the teacher-researcher (so called because the pupils are being taught as well as observed; i.e. they are not simply being tested), uses a questioning approach. This serves both to facilitate learning and to reveal aspects of pupils' mathematical approaches and understanding. The case study synopsis represents an abbreviated picture of the teaching and learning that took place. For example, dialogue between pupils is omitted. The interpretation of pupils' responses is interwoven in the text and makes use of the structure of abilities discussed in Chapter 1.

Introduction

General context

Case study synopsis

The case study was undertaken in a Roman Catholic primary school in a largely urban environment: approximately 370 boys and girls on roll.

Specific context

The teacher-researcher is working with a group of five 10-year-olds. Their current topic is 'factors of numbers', and after an initial discussion with both the pupils and the regular class teacher it seemed appropriate to extend the pupils by working towards a theory for knowing when all the factors of a number have been found. Once again exact time intervals are not indicated, but overall the pupils spent approximately an hour with the teacher-researcher. Spaces in the text separate pieces of dialogue and usually also signify a time interval.

As before, in what follows the teacher-researcher's comments are preceded by a **T**. The pupils' comments are preceded by their names: Angela, Anthony, Rebecca, Martin and Katy. Other comments are in italics and, specifically, any interpretation of mathematical abilities is shown in bold italics. Pupil writing is shown in a handwriting font.

T: What do you do in order to find the factors of a number?

Martin: You start from 1 and times them and don't go past halfway.

T: Do you agree with that? Are you happy with that idea?

Agreement is indicated with a show of nodding heads.

T: Show me by writing down your method for finding the factors of 16.

T: Katy, you've got a different approach.

Katy had written:

$$16 \div 1 = 16$$
$$16 \div 2 = 8$$
$$16 \div 3 =$$
$$16 \div 4 = 4$$
$$16 \div 5 =$$
$$16 \div 6 =$$
$$16 \div 7 =$$
$$16 \div 8 = 2 \qquad \text{16, 1, 8, 2 and 4 are the factors of 16.}$$

T: That's interesting. The first thing I would say is that all of these numbers go into 16. Doesn't that mean they are all factors?

Katy: No, because 5 will not go into 16 equally. Nor will 7.

T: So they must go in exactly?

Katy: Yes.

Katy has confidently adopted an alternative method to the one intimated in the opening discussion.

T: Rebecca, can you read out what you've written down?

Rebecca: I'm showing two ways . . . the way you can times them and the way you can divide them . . . to find the factors.

Rebecca had partially written down the same as Katy above, and, additionally:

60

$$1 \times 16 = 16$$
$$2 \times 8 = 16$$
$$3 \times$$
$$4 \times 4 = 16$$

Rebecca, too, is indicating flexibility in her approach.

The discussion with Katy seemed to influence the other pupils to change the approach to which they gave their initial agreement. Anthony began by writing:

$$1 \times$$
$$2 \times$$
$$3 \times$$
$$4 \times$$
$$5 \times$$
$$6 \times$$
$$7 \times$$
$$8 \times$$

He then changed all the multiplication signs into division signs. Martin and Angela had done something similar.

Drawing the pupils together now.

T: Anthony, this is what you did to start with [*pointing to his original list above*]. I think you might have changed because you saw what other people were doing! But you possibly gave up something useful here. Let's go back to the idea of a factor. If you know 8 is a factor, do you know another factor as well?

Rebecca: Two. Two times 8 is 16.

T: So, do you agree that if you've got two numbers multiplied together giving you 16 . . . they are both factors?

A chorus of 'Yes' from the pupils.

T: So if we use the idea of multiplication to find factors rather than division . . . how would we complete Anthony's list?

The pupils collectively suggested the outcome overleaf.

$$1 \times 16 = 16$$
$$2 \times 8 = 16$$
$$3 \times$$
$$4 \times 4 = 16$$
$$5 \times$$
$$6 \times$$
$$7 \times$$
$$8 \times 2 = 16$$

Looking at the list.

T: What can we say here? We've got 2 times 8 equals 16 and 8 times 2 equals 16.

Angela: They are just reversing each other.

T: Do we need 8 times 2 equals 16?

Katy: Not really. You don't need to go past 4.

T: Well done! The question I now have is . . . is 4 halfway?

Martin: No. It's a quarter of the way.

T: To begin with there was a suggestion that we don't go past halfway . . . but we didn't go up to 8 for 16 . . . so let's investigate further to find how far we need to go with our list to find the factors of a number. Have a look at 25. But before you do, just tell me what it is that you are looking for.

Angela: Find the factors.

Katy: A way of finding them.

Anthony: When to stop.

T: Good, carry on.

*This discussion has sharpened the focus. **The pupils seem to have grasped the essential features of the problem. Mathematical reasoning has been employed to argue that pairs of products enable factors to be found and to identify those products that do not give new factors.***

T: Have you all managed to do 25? Let's have a little discussion about this. Martin, you wrote down the numbers 1 to 12. Can you say why?

Martin: It's roughly halfway.

Martin seems to be clinging to his initial theory!

T: OK. Let's have a look at what Katy has written down.

Katy had written:

$1 \times 25 = 25$

$2 \times$

$3 \times$

$4 \times$

$5 \times 5 = 25$

$6 \times$

$7 \times$

$8 \times$

$9 \times$

$10 \times$ 25, 1 and 5 are factors of 25.

T: What's the line for Katy?

Katy: There are no more factors to find. There's only 1, 25 and 5.

T: Now we certainly didn't need to go halfway.

Katy: We went a fifth of the way.

T: And for 16 you went . . .?

Rebecca: A quarter of the way.

T: That's interesting isn't it? Let's try 36 next. What would be your idea now? Are you going to write down 1 to halfway? Have you got a way of predicting how far to go?

Angela: It'll be a sixth of the way, because it was a quarter then it was a fifth.

T: Test it and see what happens.

A new strategy for knowing when to stop writing down product pairs has been conjectured. The basis of the conjecture is the recognition of pattern.

T: Let's have a look now . . . together . . . at 36. What factors did you get, Anthony?

Anthony: 36, 1, 2, 18, 3, 12, 4 and 9.

Anthony had written:

$1 \times 36 = 36$

$2 \times 18 = 36$

$3 \times 12 = 36$

$4 \times 9 = 36$

$5 \times$

$6 \times 6 = 36$ Factors of 36: 36, 1, 2, 18, 3, 12, 4, 9, 6

T: The big question is, how did you know where to stop?

Katy: Because of the pattern . . . with 16 you go a quarter of the way, with 25 you go a fifth of the way, with 36 it just carries on with the pattern.

T: It does. Has anybody tried 49? Before you do . . . what's your theory? How long will your list be?

Anthony: One to 7.

Anthony and Katy have justified their thinking in terms of the emerging pattern.

The group is drawn together.

T: Martin, how did you get your list so quickly? You've got 1 times 49 and 2 times a squiggle. Why a squiggle?

Martin: Because 49 is not in the 2 times table.

T: What about 3 times a squiggle?

Martin: Because 49 is not in the 3 times table.

T: [*Turning to look at other group members*] He's got a squiggle for 4. Why?

Angela: It's even . . . 49 is odd.

T: He's got a squiggle for 5.

Rebecca: Because 49 does not end in 0 or 5.

T: And 6 . . . another squiggle.

Katy: It's even again.

The pupils are drawing on previously learnt material. They have remembered a generalised approach for deciding whether or not numbers have factors.

64

T: Then we get to 7, which is a seventh of the way down. That really was quick wasn't it? The numbers you have looked at so far are 16, 25, 36 and 49. What's special about these numbers?

The pupils give various ideas related to the sequence. For example, they proffer 'even, odd, even, odd'.

T: Let me make a suggestion. The pattern I have in mind has got something to do with their factors. What's the connection between stopping at 4 and 16?

Anthony: Four 4s are 16.

T: Can you carry this on?

Rebecca: Five 5s are 25. Six 6s are 36.

Martin: Seven 7s are 49.

T. Good. Have you seen this before?

The teacher-researcher writes:

$$4^2$$

Anthony: A squared number.

T: It equals?

Martin: Sixteen.

T: So how would you write 25?

Angela: Five squared.

T: And 49?

Angela/Anthony: Seven squared.

T: Have you come across this symbol?

The teacher-researcher writes:

$$\sqrt{}$$

Martin: On a calculator . . . square root.

T: If I write $\sqrt{49}$, what I want to know is, what number multiplied by itself is 49?

Martin/Rebecca: Seven.

T: OK. $\sqrt{25}$?

Pupils: Five.

T: $\sqrt{36}$?

Pupils: Six.

T: OK. You've got it. So how do you know where to stop? For 49 we stop at 7, but what shall we say 7 is?

Pupils: Square root of 49.

T: If we want to do 36 . . . how far would we go down with the numbers?

Pupils: Stop at 6.

T: What is 6?

Pupils: The square root of 36.

Rebecca: So whatever number you choose, go to the square root.

T: That's a good theory! You put that very well. You said that whatever number you choose . . . now I chose some special numbers . . . wouldn't it be interesting to know whether this theory works for any number?

Katy: Try it for 66. It's 8 point something.

T: OK. Try it.

The pupils have recognised another pattern built on the perceived relationship between the 'stop-number', or the point where the list of numbers stops, and the number whose factors are sought. Mathematical symbolism has been used to facilitate the expression of this awareness. The early conjecture on how far to extend the list has been refined and related to the number whose factors are sought.

T: Let's put our heads together and see what we've got.

Rebecca had written:

$$1 \times 66 = 66$$
$$2 \times 33 = 66$$
$$3 \times 22 = 66$$
$$4 \times$$
$$5 \times$$
$$6 \times 11 = 66$$
$$7 \times$$
$$8 \times \qquad 11, 6, 22, 3, 2, 33, 1, 66$$

T: Why stop at 8, Rebecca?

Rebecca: Stop at the square root of 64.

T: Let's have a quick talk about that. What are eight 8s?

Pupils: Sixty-four.

T: What are nine 9s?

Pupils: Eighty one.

T: So if eight 8s are 64, what is the square root of 64?

Pupils: Eight.

T: If nine 9s are 81, what is the square root of 81?

Pupils: Nine.

T: What can we say about the square root of any number between 64 and 81?

Martin: Everything from 64 to 81 will be 8 point something.

T: So we could put a line between the 8 and 9 to show that's where the square root is. Do a write-up now and show how to find the factors of 32.

Angela wrote:

Finding Factors

To find the factors of a number I would run through the times tables in my head and if that number was the answer of say a sum in the two times table then two would be a factor. If you wanted to find the factors of an even number two is definitely one of its factors. To find out when to stop you have to find the square root of that number. It isn't necessary to carry on after the square root because you will just be repeating the sums in reverse order and you will already have those answers somewhere at the beginning. My method for finding the factors of 32 would be this.

$$1 \times 32 = 32$$
$$2 \times 16 = 32$$
$$3 \times \sim = 32$$
$$4 \times 8 = 32$$
$$5 \times \sim = 32$$

I have stopped at five because 32's square root is 5. ? 32's square root is somewhere in between five and six.

Angela has generalised her method and justified her approach with sound mathematical reasoning.

Conclusion

In keeping with the comments at the end of Chapter 6, forms of teacher–pupil interaction and the nature of challenge offered to pupils are revealed through case studies of this kind. Collection of evidence along this lines by teachers can provide a valuable basis for discussion about the forms of provision for able pupils that they consider to be the most appropriate.

Chapter 9

A note on mathematical achievement and gender

In 1982 the Cockcroft Report summarised the relative performance of boys and girls in the following terms:

> A smaller proportion of girls than boys enter for O-level mathematics; of those who do enter, a smaller proportion of girls achieve high grades, and of those with high grades, a smaller proportion of girls than boys proceed to A-level. The result of this is that nearly three times as many boys as girls entered for A-level mathematics in 1979. (Cockroft 1982: 276, para B8).

In the past 20 years, the performance of girls relative to boys has improved. First, the proportion of girls and boys entering for GCSE mathematics is now more evenly balanced (Table 9.1). Secondly, the proportion of girls achieving grades A to C is similar to that for boys (Table 9.2).

Table 9.1 Entry to GCSE mathematics

Year	Boys	Girls
2000	50.3%	49.7%

Table 9.2 Proportion of entry to GCSE mathematics achieving grades A to C

Year	Boys	Girls
2000	46.7%	47.6%

In 1979 the proportions for GCE grade A passes were 5.5% and 2.6% for boys and girls, respectively, a ratio of approximately two to one. The corresponding figures for 2000 are given in Table 9.3. In 1979 approximately three times as many boys as girls went on to take A-level mathematics. Data for 2000 indicates that this ratio has fallen from three to one to less than two to one (Table 9.4).

Table 9.3 Proportion of pupils achieving grade A* or A

Year	Boys	Girls
2000	9.6%	9.1%

Table 9.4 Number of entries to GCE A-level mathematics ('000s)

Year	Boys	Girls
2000	38	22

Table 9.5 Proportions of entries to A-level mathematics achieving grade A.

Year	Boys	Girls
2000	29%	30%

At the highest grades in 1979, boys were more successful: 15.4% of boys obtained a grade A pass in A-level mathematics compared with 10.1% of girls. The corresponding figures for 2000 are shown in Table 9.5.

Taking a wider view, the 2000 figures show that 64% of boys and 68% of girls achieved A-level grades A to C. Although these figures indicate an improvement in the performance of girls relative to boys, it must be remembered that in absolute terms more boys than girls achieve these high grades.

It is interesting to note the strong gender imbalance in higher education courses. The proportions of female students graduating with mathematical science degrees is shown in Table 9.6.

Table 9.6 Percentage of female students graduating with mathematical science degrees

Year	Undergraduate	Postgraduate
2000	39%	30%

Conclusion

In general terms it seems that the performance of girls relative to boys in public examinations has improved. However, able girls are still not choosing to study mathematics in the same numbers as boys beyond the age of 16.

Sources for data: OFSTED PANDAs; DfEE; Higher Education Statistics Agency, www.hesa.ac.uk (accessed July 2001).

Chapter 10

Conclusion

A few key points are emphasised below:

1. In considering the most appropriate forms of provision for mathematically able children it seems important to keep in mind the nature of the mathematical abilities we are trying to develop. The work of Krutetskii and others provides a valuable starting point for discussion and is summarised below.

   Able children aged approximately 11 and over have the ability to:
   - grasp the formal structure of a problem in a way that leads to ideas for action – *establish the direction of the problem;*
   - generalise from the study of examples; *search for and recognise pattern; explore special cases in a systematic way leading to conjectures about possible relationships;* generalise approaches to problem solving;
   - reason in a logical way and as a consequence develop chains of reasoning: *explaining, verifying, justifying, proving;*
   - use mathematical symbols as part of the thinking process; *represent mathematical situations using algebraic notation;*
   - think flexibly; adapt their ways of approaching problems and to switch from one mode of thought to another;
   - reverse their direction of thought; work forwards and backwards in an attempt to solve a problem;
   - leave out intermediate steps in a logical argument and think in abbreviated mathematical forms; *take valid shortcuts;*
   - remember generalised mathematical relationships, problem types, generalised ways of approaching problems and patterns of reasoning; *utilise relational thinking.*

2. A *discerning* classroom based approach to the provision of challenge is one that simultaneously recognises and promotes mathematical ability.

3. Challenge can be provided through:
- problem solving, enquiry and a focus on mathematical proof;
- mathematical discussion, the initiation of sustained dialogue in which questioning by the teacher promotes the growth of pupils' mathematical abilities and understanding.

4. Organisational approaches can support the provision of challenge through:
- team approaches to planning and the design of programmes of study that seek to *build* challenge in;
- developing criteria for the selection of challenging materials including the most effective way to utilise commercially available schemes;
- puzzle and problem displays;
- leadership that creates a consensus through review meetings and co-teaching;
- enlivening the curriculum with *extra challenge* via a mathematics club, maths and logic festivals, competitions and quizzes, industry links and mathematical magazines.

5. The way children are grouped *per se* will not guarantee that they are challenged.

6. Case studies that reveal the context and nature of children's mathematical thinking provide a valuable resource for teachers seeking to achieve agreement about the most appropriate forms of provision.

Chapter 11

A note on resources

This chapter offers some suggestions about published resources for able children. The intention behind this compilation of resources is to provide teachers with a *starting point* rather than an exhaustive list. For example, there are a large number of commercially available schemes but not all of them are mentioned below. Omission from the list should not be taken as an implied criticism! It is the approach to commercially available schemes that is important (see 'Published schemes', p. 39), and with able children in mind it seems appropriate to select elements of schemes that claim to provide challenge or that facilitate the planning of challenge. In the references to schemes that follow, these elements are identified. Additional ideas for resources can be found in 'Extra challenge' (p. 42). However, the first place to look for challenging activities is in the relevant sections of the NNS Frameworks.

Primary resources

- *Framework for Teaching Mathematics from Reception to Year 6* (DfEE 1999), 'Solving problems' strand.
- See also 'Reasoning about numbers with challenges and simplifications' (1999) from the five-day course materials or the 'red box'.

Schemes

1. BEAM, 'Starting From' series.
   BEAM Education Ltd, Maze Workshops, 72A Southgate Road, London, N1 3JT (Tel.: 02076 843323), www.beam.co.uk

2. Cambridge Mathematics Direct series.
   Lesson plans contain extension suggestions under 'Pupil activities' (Key Stages 1 and 2).
   Cambridge University Press, The Edinburgh Building, Shaftesbury Road, Cambridge, CB2 2RU (Tel.: 01223 325013), http://uk.cambridge.org/education/

3. Rigby:
- *Maths Pyramid: Challenging More Able Children in the Daily Mathematics Lesson*. Teacher's book for each year from Reception to Year 6.
- *Numeracy Focus: Problem of the Week*. Years 1 to 6.
  Rigby Educational Publishers (Tel.: 01865 888044),
  www.rigbyed.co.uk

4. Prim-Ed Publishing:
- *Maths Problems Galore*.
  Problem Solving with Maths series.
  Prim-Ed Publishing, PO Box 051, Nuneaton, Warwickshire,
  CV11 6ZU, www.prim-ed.com

5. *Solving Problems R to Y6*, H. Koll and S. Mills (2000).
   A. & C. Black, London (Tel.: 02077 580200), www.acblack.co.uk

6. Ginn & Company:
- *New Abacus 2–6*, R. Merttens and D. Kirkby.
- Numeracy Extras series: *Maths Express* and *Numeracy Lessons –* Lessons for Years 1–6, with extension ideas.
  Ginn & Company, Linacre House, Jordan Hill, Oxford, OX2 8DP
  (Tel.: 01865 888000), www.ginn.co.uk

7. *Maths Plus: Solving Problems, Years 3–6*, R. Griffiths (2000).
   Heinemann Education, PO Box 381, Oxford, OX2 8BR
   (Tel.: 01865 888020), www.heinemann.co.uk

Non-scheme-based resources

1. Association of Teachers of Mathematics (ATM):
- *Exploring Mathematics with Younger Children*, ATM.
- *Primary Points of Departure*, ATM.
  Association of Teachers of Mathematics Publications,
  7 Shaftesbury Street, Derby, DE23 8YB (Tel.: 01332 346599),
  www.atm.org.uk Ask for their catalogue for more ideas on
  possible resources.

2. *Domino Puzzles*, D. Fielker (2000).
   BEAM Education Ltd, Maze Workshops, 72A Southgate Road,
   London, N1 3JT (Tel.: 02076 843323), www.beam.co.uk

3. Cambridge University Press:
- *Playing With Numbers: Puzzles for the Daily Mathematics Lesson*,
  M. Cornelius (2001).
- *Talking Points in Mathematics*, A. Straker (1993).
  Cambridge University Press, The Edinburgh Building,
  Shaftesbury Road, Cambridge, CB2 2RU (Tel.: 01223 325013),
  http://uk.cambridge.org/education/

4. Claire Publications:
- *Challenges for Children: Problem Solving for Young Children,* S. Hyams (1989).
- *Maths to Think About,* N. Graham and R. Timm (2000).
  Claire Publications, Unit 8, Tey Brook Craft Centre, Great Tey, Colchester, Essex, CO6 1JE, www.clairepublications.com

5. *Investigations and Problem Solving,* O. El-Naggar (1995).
   QEd, The Rom Building, Eastern Avenue, Lichfield, Staffs, WS13 6RN.

- *Framework for Teaching Mathematics: Years 7, 8 and 9* (DfEE 2001) 'Using and applying mathematics to solve problems'.

Secondary resources

Schemes

1. CAME Project (1998)
   CAME stands for Cognitive Acceleration in Mathematics Education. It is not specifically for more able pupils, but offers many demanding lessons related to process abilities and links between content areas. A Key Stage 3 resource.
   Heinemann Education, PO Box 381, Oxford, OX2 8BR (Tel.: 01865 888020), www.heinemann.co.uk

2. Mathematics Enhancement Project (MEP)
   A Key Stage 4 resource offering 'express' and 'special' routes for higher-level pupils working towards grades A* and A, respectively.
   CIMT, School of Education, University of Exeter, Exeter, EX1 2LU, (Tel.: 01392 217113), www.intermep.org

3. Key Maths
   Look in the teacher's file for supplementary ideas that occasionally offer suggestions for stretching more able pupils, as does guidance under Ma1. See also the homework extensions.
   Nelson Thornes Ltd., Delta Place, 27 Bath Road, Cheltenham, GL53 7TH (Tel.: 01242 267100), www.nelsonthornes.co.uk

Non-scheme-based resources

1. Mathematical Association:
- *Are You Sure? Learning about Proof* (1999).
- *Can You Prove It?* (2000). Developing concepts of proof in primary and secondary schools.

- *Problem Pages* (2000). A photocopiable book of thought-provoking mathematics problems for sixth-form and upper secondary school students.
Mathematical Association, 259 London Road, Leicester, LE2 3BE. (Tel.: 01162 210013), www.m-a.org.uk Ask for their catalogue for more ideas.

2. *Maths Challenge Books 1 to 3*, T. Gardiner (2000), Oxford University Press, www.oup.com

3. *The Crest of the Peacock*, G. Joseph (1991), Non European Roots of Mathematics, I B Tauris, London.

4. *Fermat's Last Theorem*, S. Singh (1998), Fourth Estate, London.

5. Shell Centre:
- *Journey into Mathematics, Teacher's Guide 1*, Key Stage 3, A. Bell (1978).
- *Journey into Mathematics, Teacher's Guide 2*, Key Stage 3, A. Bell (1979).
- *Problems with Patterns and Numbers* (1984).
- *Extended Tasks for GCSE Mathematics*, S. Madden and R. Crust (1989).
Shell Centre Publications, University of Nottingham. See their website for more resources at www.mathshell.com

6. *Mathematical Investigations in Your Classroom*, S. Pirie (1987), Macmillan, London.

7. SMILE:
- Problem-solving activities (National Curriculum levels 6 to 8)
- Problem-solving posters (National Curriculum levels 4 to 8)
- Activities for maths clubs (level 2 to exceptional performance)
- Multicultural mathematical activities (levels 5 to 7)
- MICROSMILE: Mathematical Puzzles
SMILE, Isaac Newton Centere, 108A Lancaster Road, London, W11 1QS (Tel.: 02075 984841), www.smilemaths.co.uk

8. *Autograph.* Geometrical software. See Introductory exercises for investigational starting points with occasional extension tasks for more able pupils. More details at www.autograph-maths.com

Primary and secondary resources

1. Tarquin Mathematics:
   Look in their catalogue for enrichment material and logical thinking.
   Tarquin Publications, Stradbroke, Diss, Norfolk, IP21 5JP (Tel.: 01379 384218).

2. *Maths Problems For Gifted and Talented Students*, J. Murchinson (1996). Suitable for junior to mid-secondary years.
   Phoenix Education.

3. Association of Teachers of Mathematics
   - Points of Departure Booklets 1 to 4; various posters and much more!
   - *Eight Days a Week*, C. Bills (ed.) (2000). Puzzles, problems and questions to activate the mind.
     Association of Teachers of Mathematics Publications,
     7 Shaftesbury Street, Derby, DE23 8YB (Tel.: 01332 346599),
     www.atm.org.uk

4. *Problem Solving Through Investigation Books 1–3*. For pupils aged 9–12.
   Prim-Ed Publishing, PO Box 051, Nuneaton, Warwickshire,
   CV11 6ZU, www.prim-ed.com

5. *Board Games Round the World: A Resource Book for Mathematical Investigations*, R. Bell and M. Cornelius (1988).
   Cambridge University Press, The Edinburgh Building,
   Shaftesbury Road, Cambridge, CB2 2RU (Tel.: 01223 325013),
   http://uk.cambridge.org/education/

6. Blackwell:
   - *Sources of Mathematical Discovery*, L. Mottershead (1977).
   - *Thinking Things Through*, L. Burton (1988).

Websites for enrichment activities

NRICH Online Maths Project   http://nrich.maths.org.uk

Internet Resources 2001, compiled   www.argonet.co.uk/oundlesch
by the ICT Training Centre,
Oundle School, Peterborough

References

Bell, A. *et al.* (1978), *Journey into Mathematics: Teacher's Guide 1.* Nottingham: Shell Centre Publications, University of Nottingham.

Bell, A. *et al.* (1979), *Journey into Mathematics: Teacher's Guide 2.* Nottingham: Shell Centre Publications, University of Nottingham.

Black, P. and Wiliam, D. (1998) *Inside the Black Box: Raising Standards through Classroom Assessment.* London: King's College.

Chyriwsky, M. and Kennard, R. (1997) 'Attitudes to able children: a survey of mathematics teachers in English secondary schools', *High Ability Studies* 8, 47–59.

Cockcroft, W. (1982) *Mathematics Counts: Report of the Committee of Inquiry into the Teaching of Mathematics under the Chairmanship of Dr. W. H. Cockroft.* London: HMSO.

Denton, C. and Postlethwaite, K. (1985) *Able Children: Identifying Them in the Classroom.* Windsor: NFER-Nelson.

Department of Education and Science (DES) (1985) *Mathematics from 5 to 16.* London: HMSO.

Department for Education and Employment (DfEE) (1999) *Framework for Teaching Mathematics from Reception to Year 6.* The National Numeracy Strategy. London: DfEE.

Department for Education and Employment (DfEE) (2000a) *Excellence in Cities Phase 2, Paper 2.* London: DfEE.

Department for Education and Employment (DfEE) (2000b) *Mathematical Challenges for Able Pupils in Key Stages 1 and 2.* London: DfEE.

Department for Education and Employment (DfEE) (2000c) *National Literacy and Numeracy Strategies: Guidance on Teaching Able Children.* London: DfEE.

Department for Education and Employment (DfEE) (2001) *Framework for Teaching Mathematics: Years 7, 8 and 9.* The National Numeracy Strategy. London: DfEE.

Department for Education and Employment (DfEE)/Qualifications and Curriculum Authority (QCA) (1999) *Mathematics: The National Curriculum for England.* London: The Stationery Office.

Fielker, D. (1997) *Extending Mathematical Ability Through Whole Class Teaching.* London: Hodder and Stoughton.

Freeman, J. (1991) *Gifted Children Growing Up.* London: Cassell.

Freeman, J. (1998) *Educating the Very Able: Current International Research.* London: The Stationery Office.

Gardner, M. (1993) *Frames of Mind: The Theory of Multiple Intelligences*, second edition. New York: Basic Books.

Gross, M. (1993) *Exceptionally Gifted Children.* London: Routledge.

Her Majesty's Inspectorate of Schools (HMI) (1978) *Primary Education In England: A Survey by HM Inspectors of Schools.* London: HMSO.

Her Majesty's Inspectorate of Schools (HMI) (1979) *Aspects of Secondary Education in England: A Survey by HM Inspectors of Schools.* London: HMSO.

Her Majesty's Inspectorate of Schools (HMI) (1985) *Mathematics from 5 to 16.* London: DES.

Her Majesty's Inspectorate of Schools (HMI) (1992) *The Education of Very Able Children in Maintained Schools.* London: HMSO.

Jones, E. D. and Southern, W. (1991) 'Conclusions About Acceleration: Echoes of Debate', in Jones, E. D. and Southern, W. (eds) *The Academic Acceleration of Gifted Children.* New York: Teachers College Press.

Kennard, R. (1992) Cultures Count, *Century Mathematics (Theme Materials).* Cheltenham: Stanley Thornes.

Kerry, T. (1981) *Teaching Bright Pupils in Mixed Ability Classes: A Self-instructional Handbook of Strategies and Suggestions.* Basingstoke: Macmillan.

Krutetskii, V. A. (1976) *The Psychology of Mathematical Abilities in Schoolchildren.* Chicago, IL: University of Chicago Press.

Mason, J. (1985) *Thinking Mathematically.* Wokingham: Addison-Wesley.

National Commission on Education (1993) *Learning to Succeed: The Way Ahead.* Oxford: Paul Hamlyn Foundation.

Office for Standards in Education (OFSTED) (1994) *Science and Mathematics in Schools. A Review.* London: HMSO.

Office for Standards in Education (OFSTED) (1995) *Mathematics. A review of inspection findings 1993/94.* London: HMSO.

Office for Standards in Education (OFSTED) (1998) *Secondary Education 1993-1997: A Review of Secondary Schools in England.* London: The Stationery Office.

Office for Standards in Education (OFSTED) (1999a) Primary Education 1994-98. *A Review of Primary Schools in England.* London: The Stationery Office.

Office for Standards in Education (OFSTED) (1999b) *Standards in the Secondary Curriculum 1997/98: Mathematics.* London: OFSTED.

Open University (1986) *Girls into Mathematics.* Cambridge: Cambridge University Press.

Osborn, H. H. (1983) 'The assessment of mathematical abilities', *Educational Research* **25**(1), 28–40.

Pirie, S. (1987) *Mathematical Investigations in Your Classroom.* Basingstoke: Macmillan.

Presmeg, N. (1986) 'Visualisation and mathematical giftedness', *Educational Studies in Mathematics* **17**(3), 297–311.

Qualifications and Curriculum Authority (QCA) (forthcoming) *Exemplification Matierals Supporting Gifted and Talented Pupils.*

Renzulli, J. S. (1986) 'The three ring conception of giftedness', in Sternberg, R. and Davidson, J. E. (eds) *Conceptions of Giftedness.* Cambridge: Cambridge University Press.

Research for the Education of Able Pupils (REACH) Project (Research for the Education of Able Pupils), University of Sunderland (Discontinued).

Sukhnandan, L. (1998) *Streamimg, Setting and Grouping by Ability: A Review of the Literature.* Slough: NFER.

Shuard, H. (1986) *Primary Mathematics Today and Tomorrow.* Harlow: Longman.

Skemp, R. (1979) *Intelligence, Learning and Action.* Chichester: John Wiley.

Span, P. and Overtoom-Corsmit, R. (1986) 'Information processing', *Educational Studies in Mathematics* **17**(3), 273–95.

Stanley, J. C. (1990) 'Finding and helping young people with exceptional mathematical reasoning ability', in Howe, M. J. A (ed.) *Encouraging the Development of Exceptional Skills and Talents.* British Psychological Society.

Straker, A. (1983) *Mathematics for Gifted Pupils.* Harlow: Longman.

UK Mathematics Foundation (2000) *Acceleration or Enrichment?* Birmingham: School of Mathematics, University of Birmingham.

Printed in the United Kingdom
by Lightning Source UK Ltd.
107631UKS00002B/523-538